Sources for Library Materials in FY09
Albany County Public Library

■ Cash Gifts
■ Public Money
  Donated Items

2.6%

45.0%

52.5%

"There are some stories that need to be told and never forgotten. The events that began on October 2, 2006, when a lone shooter started firing his shotgun at ten innocent Amish schoolgirls in a one-room schoolhouse is one of those stories. It could have ended there and forever transformed a tight-knit Amish community from one of love and trust to fear and hate—instead it changed the way the world would think about forgiveness, family, and community.

In an era of nonstop litigation and in which people demand their 'pound of flesh' for any real or perceived offense, *Think No Evil* is a timely reminder that there is a better way that the world has forgotten. The author's Amish background gave him unique access and special insight into how the Amish were able to extend absolute forgiveness to the man who killed their children and embrace that man's family as one of their own.

You will not be able to look at life the same way after reading this book."
                                 —Glenn Beck, radio and television host and
                                 number one *New York Times* bestselling author

"In the pages of this book Jonas tells the painful events that hit the Amish community in October 2006. You share their shock as he explains how the event unfolded and rocked their community in Nickel Mines, Pennsylvania, the outlying areas, and the entire nation as it spread throughout the media. Being raised Amish, Jonas has a special way of sharing with us how forgiveness is taught from childhood. This is the story of forgiveness. How the community forgave and how Jonas himself in his personal life has forgiven without blame or vengeance and how it has brought healing personally and in the entire community."
                                 —Dr. Richard D. Dobbins, pastor, psychologist, author,
                                 and founder of EMERGE Ministries

"We were shocked by the heinous crime. It was beyond belief. But when the Amish community quickly forgave, we were mystified. How could they do that? Why would they do that?

How can we forgive those that have wounded us? What about the reoccurring emotions? What about 'forgive and forget'? Forgiveness is hard yet we all have people in our lives we need to forgive. What can we learn from this story?

Jonas Beiler lifts the curtain and lets us see behind the scenes. It is an amazing story of God's grace and forgiveness as a way of life working through shattered lives to heal and restore. And he courageously lifts the curtain on his own life and tragic events that lends authenticity to the truth so vividly portrayed by the Amish families. We cannot dismiss this story as irrelevant to us."

—Ruth Graham, daughter of Rev. Billy Graham

"A clear road map for achieving the relative peace and contentment that many seek! Jonas's deep understanding of forgiveness and its freeing power provides a window into the discipline and courage the Amish community has taught and modeled for numerous generations. You are left contemplating what a different world we could create if more of us would be willing to choose a personal path of peace through forgiveness."

—Samuel R. Beiler, president/CEO of Auntie Anne's Pretzels

"This is a dramatic story of the most unthinkable evil and the triumph over it through forgiveness—a story portraying the very lowest and highest of human conduct. Jonas Beiler captures the gut-wrenching experience of a community having to come to terms with an episode of homegrown violence that will never be understood or explained. He portrays the Amish, who are at the center of this drama, as real people who struggle with grief and anger like the rest of us, yet who rose above it through faith to offer a healing forgiveness. There is much in *Think No Evil* to inspire a new approach to conflict and violence around the world."

—Don Eberly, two-time White House presidential aide, award-winning author, and advocate for community solutions

"If there's anybody who has lived a life of forgiveness, it is Jonas Beiler. This forgiveness grew out of the theology of growing up in an Amish home. He and Anne have been dear friends for several years now, and it is great to see them live out the theology of forgiveness in their everyday lives."

—Bill Gaither, songwriter

"Many accuse our Amish neighbors of being strange and unusual. In the immediate aftermath of the Nickel Mines school shootings, the world found that to be true. The deeply hurting Amish community showed a strange and unusual commitment to show deep grace, mercy, and forgiveness . . . of the type that should be normal and usual for us all. Jonas Beiler takes us into the story of the Nickel Mines shootings, offering readers deep insights into how the world should be. This is a compelling story that will not only make you think but just might change your life."

—Dr. Walt Mueller, president of Center for Parent/ Youth Understanding, Elizabethtown, Pennsylvania, and author of *Engaging the Soul of Youth Culture*

THINK

INSIDE THE STORY
OF THE AMISH
SCHOOLHOUSE
SHOOTING...
AND BEYOND

NO EVIL

JONAS BEILER WITH
SHAWN SMUCKER

HOWARD BOOKS
A DIVISION OF SIMON & SCHUSTER
New York   London   Toronto   Sydney

Our purpose at Howard Books is to:
- *Increase faith* in the hearts of growing Christians
- *Inspire holiness* in the lives of believers
- *Instill hope* in the hearts of struggling people everywhere
Because He's coming again!

HOWARD
BOOKS

Published by Howard Books, a division of Simon & Schuster, Inc.
1230 Avenue of the Americas, New York, NY 10020
www.howardpublishing.com

Think No Evil © 2009 Jonas Beiler

Published in association with Ambassador Literary Agency, Nashville, Tennessee

Library of Congress Cataloging-in-Publication Data is available

ISBN 978-1-4165-6298-6

1   3   5   7   9   10   8   6   4   2

HOWARD and colophon are registered trademarks of Simon & Schuster, Inc.

Manufactured in the United States of America

For information regarding special discounts for bulk purchases, please contact:
Simon & Schuster Special Sales at 1-866-506-1949
or business@simonandschuster.com.

The Simon & Schuster Speakers Bureau can bring authors to your live event.
For more information or to book an event, contact the Simon & Schuster Speakers
Bureau at 1-866-248-3049 or visit our website at www.simonspeakers.com.

Edited by Cindy Lambert
Interior design by Davina Mock-Maniscalco
Photography by Tim Landis. Used by permission. All rights reserved.

I would like to dedicate this book to the community
of Nickel Mines, Pennsylvania, and the people who
have been forever changed by such a horrific event,
the families who lost precious children,
the first responders, and the pastors
and counselors who showed up
immediately to support this community.
To those who will continue to mourn
and choose to forgive every day,
my prayer is that you will find yourself
on a path of recovery and that a new normal
will bring with it some measure of redemption.
May God's grace be with all who struggle to forgive
and those who long to be forgiven.

CONTENTS

Nickel Mines Schoolhouse

CHAPTER ONE

Gates Wide Open

IT HAS BECOME numbingly familiar: A man walks into a church, a store, a dormitory, a nursing home, or a school, and begins shooting. Sometimes there is panic, sometimes there is an eerie quietness. But always bodies fall, almost in unison, with the shell casings dropping from the gun. And always there is death. Senseless, inexplicable loss of innocent life. Within seconds we receive reports on our BlackBerries or iPhones. Within minutes the shooting is "Breaking News" on CNN, and by the end of the day it has seared a name in our memories. *Columbine. Virginia Tech.*

Or for me, the Amish schoolhouse shooting.

As I write this, it has been nearly three years since our community watched as ten little girls were carried out of their one-room school and laid on the grass where first responders desperately tried to save their lives. As a professional counselor and the founder of a counseling center that serves central Pennsylvania, I saw firsthand the effects this traumatic event had on our citizens. And as someone who grew up in an Amish household and suffered through my own share of tragedies, I found myself strangely drawn back into a culture that I once chose to leave. I know these people, who still travel by horse and buggy and light their homes with gas lanterns, yet as I moved among them during this tragedy I found myself asking questions: How were they able to cope so well with the loss of their children? What enables a father who lost two daughters in that schoolhouse to bear no malice toward the man who shot them? And what can I learn—what can *we* learn—to help us more gracefully carry our own life burdens?

That last question is what prompted me to share what I have learned from the families who lost so much that day. The Amish will be the first to tell you they're not perfect. But they do a lot of things right. Forgiveness is one of them. In my counseling I have seen how lesser tragedies destroy relationships, ruin marriages, and turn people's hearts to stone. Life throws so much at us that seems unfair and undeserved, and certainly the shootings at the Amish schoolhouse in Nickel Mines, Pennsylvania, were both. And yet not a word of anger or retribution from the Amish. Somehow they have learned that blame and vengeance are toxic, while forgiveness and reconciliation disarm their grief. Even in the valley of the shadow of death they know how to live well, and that is the story I want to share—how ordinary human beings ease their own pain by forgiving those who have hurt them.

It is a story that began decades ago, when I knew it was time to choose.

LITTLE HAS changed in Lancaster County, Pennsylvania, from the time I was a young boy to that fateful October day when shots pierced the stillness of our countryside. Towns like Cedar Lane, New Holland, Gap, and Iva might have grown slightly, but as you drive through the hills and valleys along White Oak Road or Buck Hill Road, you'll see the same quaint farms and patchwork fields that the Amish have worked for generations. Like most Amish boys, I learned to read in a little one-room schoolhouse and could hitch up a team of horses by the time I was twelve years old. I didn't feel deprived by our lack of electricity or phones, and it didn't really bother me to wear the plain clothes that set us apart from my non-Amish friends. As far as I was concerned, being Amish was fine with me, except for one thing: I loved cars. I mean, I really loved them. I couldn't imagine never being able to drive one, but I knew that's what was at stake if I remained Amish.

In Amish culture, you may be born into an Amish family, but you must choose for yourself if you want to be Amish, and that usually happens somewhere between the ages of sixteen and twenty-one. You may have seen documentaries about Amish teenagers sowing their wild oats for a year or so before deciding to leave or stay within the Amish faith. While it's true that Amish young people are given their freedom, in reality few teenagers stray very far from the Amish way of life. But all eventually must choose, and once you decide to stay and become baptized as Amish you can never leave without serious consequences, including being shunned by other Amish, even your own parents and relatives. I couldn't imagine leaving my loving family, but I also felt a tug to explore life beyond my Amish roots. I worried that it would hurt my father if I chose to leave. I remember once asking my dad why we did the things we did, and he told me it was all about choice. We choose to live the way we do. It is not forced upon us. So when I finally told him, at age fifteen, that I did not want to stay Amish, I know he was disappointed, but he was not harsh with me, nor did he try to talk me out of it. He respected my choice, which has profoundly shaped my thinking about the Amish.

You can always trust the Amish. They live up to their word. If they say they will do something, they will do it. You may have heard the expression, "Do as I say, not as I do." Well, you would never hear that from Amish parents. Whatever they teach their children, they back it up with their actions. My dad told me we had a choice, and when I made a choice that he obviously wished I hadn't made, he did not turn his back on me. He taught me an important lesson the way most Amish teach their children: by example. Many years later, in the wake of the tragic shooting, I would see Amish mothers and fathers teach their children about forgiveness the same way.

I left the Amish community, but I never left my family, nor

did they abandon me. Because of that, I too would learn about forgiveness from my father's example. Most of my brothers and sisters made the same decision to leave for their own reasons. But my parents remained Amish, and much of my worldview is still seen through the metaphorical front windscreen of an Amish buggy.

During those winter months after the shooting, so much of our community was covered in stillness. The shortened days felt somber and subdued as we were constantly reminded of the girls who had perished. Normally, the sights and sounds surrounding my home in Lancaster County filled me with a sense of nostalgia; the rhythm of horse and buggies clip-clopping their way down our backcountry roads, or the sight of children dashing home from school through a cold afternoon, had always been pleasant reminders to me of growing up as a young Amish boy. But that feeling of nostalgia had been replaced with a solemn feeling of remembrance.

Lancaster County is a unique community, the kind which seems rarely to exist in America anymore. Many of my friends come from families that have lived in this same area for over two hundred years, some even from the time before our country was formed—often we are still connected by friendships held long ago by our parents, our grandparents, or our great-grandparents. You will find roadside stands selling produce or baked goods, and it is not unusual for them to be left unattended, the prices listed on a bucket or a box where you can leave payment for the goods you take. The vast majority of the county is farmland, and in the summer, various shades of green spread out to the horizon. Beautiful forests line the hills and drift down to waving fields of corn and tobacco and hay.

In the fall months many of the small towns sponsor fairs or festivals, some established for seventy-five years or more. They were originally conceived for local farmers to bring and sell their harvested goods, but, like much of the commerce in this area, they were also social events—an opportunity to catch up with friends you hadn't seen in a while. I can imagine that back in the day they were joyous times, the crops having been brought in, the community coming together to prepare for a long winter. Nowadays we still go to the fair every year and sit on the same street corner with all of our friends, some of whom we haven't seen all year but can count on seeing at the fair. The parade goes by, filled with local high school bands and hay wagons advertising local businesses. Our grandchildren vanish into the backstreets together, another generation of friendships created while riding the Ferris wheel or going through the haunted house. I like to think that in thirty years they will be sitting on that corner, with their children running off to ride the rides with my friends' great-grandchildren.

The Amish people live easily among us: good neighbors, hard workers—a peaceful people. They attend the same fairs with their children. Their separateness goes only as far as their plain clothing, or their lack of modern conveniences such as telephones and electricity, or the fact that they have their own schools. I have many good friends who are Amish. While they choose to live their lives free of cell phones and computers, they still walk alongside us. They mourn with us when we lose loved ones, and we with them. We talk to them about world events. They volunteer for our local fire brigades and ambulance crews, and run businesses within our community.

When the media converged on our community on that tragic October day, I guess I was an ideal person for the media to talk to: someone who grew up in the Amish community, now a family counselor familiar with the effects of grief and tragedy on people's lives. So I served as a contact for the media, doing countless interviews and sitting on various panels, almost all of which discussed the Amish response of forgiveness. It immediately became the theme for the media and the millions of people who watched in their homes or listened in their cars—this unbelievable ability to forgive the murderer of innocent children. But tragedy can change a community, and I wondered how the acts of one man would change ours.

Like many individuals, I had already experienced my share of personal turmoil over things I could not control. I knew that when these overwhelming experiences of hurt and loss occur, the very core of your being is altered. In fact, experiencing such tragedies in my life and being counseled through them led me to pursue becoming a counselor myself. Eventually I went back to school to do just that, and I studied quite a bit on my own as well. In May 1992, my wife and I opened the Family Information Center (later it became the Family Resource and Counseling Center), just up the road from Nickel Mines, a place where people from our community come to find healing from a variety of ailments, whether physical, emotional, or spiritual.

As a trained counselor I spend a lot of time listening to people pour out the pain of their lives, and can see with my own eyes how it has affected them. Nearly every time I speak with a couple whose marriage has been torn, or visit with a family who has lost a child, I am reminded that there are some hurts in life that never completely disappear.

But now, after the shooting, I understand even better how tragedies can affect individuals and communities. I think about people in places like Columbine, or the areas in the South affected by Hurricane Katrina, and I can relate to the trauma they faced and continue to live with. Our community felt shattered after the shootings in that small schoolhouse. Sometimes, as I drove those backcountry roads or stopped to talk to Amish men, I could hardly bear to think about the pain those girls' parents felt, or the innocence that our community had lost. But tragedies can also bring communities closer together if forgiveness is allowed to take hold, and if any good can come out of our loss, it is this unique practice of forgiveness that characterizes the Amish response to evil and injustice.

Word of the Amish community's decision to forgive the shooter and his family spread around the world through the media in a matter of days (ironically, from a culture with little or no access to the media). This in itself seems like a miracle to me—if you or I wanted to market a product or a concept to the entire world, we could spend millions of dollars and take years and probably still not accomplish it. Yet the Amish, who do not own phones or computers, captured the world's attention with a simple, seemingly preposterous act.

While the public was fascinated with the Amish take on forgiveness, they didn't quite know what to do with it. Some people refused to believe that anyone could offer genuine forgiveness to their children's killer. They suspected the Amish were either lying or deluding themselves. Others believed the forgiveness was genuine but thought the stoic Amish must be robotic, lacking the normal emotions experienced by you and me, to offer up such a graceful sentiment.

Neither is the case. Both misunderstandings find their origins in mainstream culture's false perception of what forgiveness truly is, and the state of mind of someone offering such unusual forgiveness. The Amish are neither liars nor zombies. They are just like you and me, and offer a sincere forgiveness with no strings attached and no dependence on any reciprocal feelings or actions. But they also hurt as deeply as the rest of us over the loss of a child or a loved one. True forgiveness is never easy, and the Amish struggle with the same emotions of anger and retribution that we all do. But they *choose* to forgive in spite of those feelings.

About a year after the shooting, I heard a story about one of the young girls who had been in the schoolhouse when the shooter entered. She was a survivor. She, along with her family and her community, had forgiven the man who killed those girls. But forgiveness does not mean that all the hurt or anger or feelings associated with the event vanish. Forgiveness, in the context of life's major disappointments and hurts, never conforms to the old Sunday-school saying, "Forgive and forget." In reality, it's next to impossible to forget an event like the shooting at her schoolhouse.

This young survivor was working in the local farmer's market when she noticed a man standing quietly off to the side of her counter. As she tried to concentrate on her work she found herself growing more and more agitated over the man's presence. He seemed to be watching all the girls behind the counter very closely, occasionally starting forward as if he were going to approach, then stopping and standing still again, always watching and fidgeting with the bag he carried with him. There was something eerie about him. Was it the way he stood, or how intently he seemed to stare at them?

All around him the farmer's market bustled with activity. The Amish were often the center of attention for first-time visitors to the market, so the Amish girl was somewhat used to being stared at, but something about this particular man made her want to hurry up and finish helping the customer she was with and then disappear into the back of the store. The difference between a curious stare and the way this stranger looked at her seemed obvious and stirred something inside her from the past.

Meanwhile, other customers walked between the long rows of stands, eyeing the goods, making their cash purchases. The vendors took the money from each sale and crammed it into old-fashioned cash registers or old money boxes. The floor was bare cement smoothed by years of wandering customers. The exposed ceiling showed iron crossbeams, pipes, and electrical wires. The whole place smelled of produce, fried food, and old books.

For many people outside Lancaster County, farmer's markets are the only place they interact with the Amish and their conservative dress—the men wearing hats, mostly black clothing with single-colored shirts, and long beards; the women with their head coverings and long hair pulled into tight buns. Amish from Pennsylvania often travel to New York City, Philadelphia, or Baltimore to sell their wares: fresh fruits and vegetables, homemade pies and cookies, quilts and handmade furniture. For some of the Amish, that is their main interaction with people outside their community as well. The Amish are hardworking, provide quality products, are almost always outgoing in that environment, and give friendly customer service.

But this particular girl, only months removed from the shooting that took place in the Nickel Mines school, got more and more nervous—she felt her breathing becoming shallow and faster, so much so that her chest rose and fell visibly. She looked around, but no one else seemed to notice the man or her reaction to his presence. Her gaze darted from here to there, first looking at him, wanting to keep an eye on him, then quickly looking away if he looked in her direction. She tried to help the customer in front of the counter, but concentrating was difficult.

Then she saw him approach. He strode forward, fishing around for something in his bag, then stuck his hand down deep and drew an object out with one fast pull.

The girl cried out and fled to the back of the stand, shaking.

The man pulled the object out of his bag and placed it on the counter. It was a Bible, a gift to the workers at the farmer's market stand. He disappeared among the hundreds of browsing shoppers. The gentleman had no idea the scare he had just given the girl. No one outside the stand had noticed that something intense had happened. Everything continued on as normal—the shoppers wandered and the vendors shouted out their sales to the lingering crowds.

But in the back, the traumatized girl wept.

Not too long before, her schoolhouse had been hemmed in by police cruisers and emergency vehicles while the sound of a handful of helicopters sliced through the sky, and the thunderous crack of rapid gunshots had echoed back at her from the rolling hills.

Forgiveness is never easy.

DURING THOSE solemn winter months following the tragedy in our community, my wife, Anne, was running errands in the countryside close to the place where the shootings had taken place. That particular area of southern Lancaster County, about sixty miles east of Philadelphia, was an alternating blanket of farms and forest. The trees stood bare. The fields in November and December and January were rock hard and flat. Where spring and summer bring deep green, and autumn blazes with color, winter often feels quiet and stark.

Anne also grew up Amish, and we both understood the questions rising within that community in the wake of the killings: Should their schools have more secure steel doors with dead bolts to keep intruders out? Should they install telephones in the one-room schoolhouses in case of emergency, a serious break from their traditional decision to shun most modern conveniences? Should the gates that guard the entrance to most of their schools' stone driveways be kept closed and locked to prevent strangers from driving onto the premises?

Anne came to a stop sign at a T in the road. She could only turn right or left. The roads rolled with the gently sloping landscape and curved along the small streams. A handful of scattered homes broke up the farmland that seemed to go on almost indefinitely. But as she paused at that intersection preparing to turn, she noticed something: directly in front of her was a one-room Amish schoolhouse, not the one where the shooting took place, but one of the many within a ten-mile radius.

Most of those schools look the same: a narrow stone or dirt lane leading from the road up to a painted cement-block building with a shingled roof and a small, covered porch; a school bell perched on the roof's peak; separate outhouses for the girls and the boys. In some of the schools' large yards you can see the outline of a base path where the children play softball. Some even have a backstop. The school grounds often take up an acre or so of land in the middle of a farmer's field, usually donated by one of the students' parents, surrounded by a three- or four-rail horse fence.

Yet there was something about this simple school that made my wife stop her car and park there for a minute. Part of it had to do with her thoughts of the children at the Nickel Mines school and all they had been through. She was also affected by visions of

13

the parents who had lost children and their long road ahead, knowing as she does how heart wrenching it is to lose a child. But on that particular day, in the wake of all the questions brought up within the Amish community about how they would deal with this disaster, there was one thing that immediately stood out.

The front gate was wide open.

We have all seen what happens in a community when people allow unforgiveness to rule their hearts. Lawsuits abound, separating the perpetrators and their families from those who were wronged, and in this separation the healing process is slowed dramatically. When forgiveness is withheld, walls are built within a community and division occurs, leading to isolation and further misunderstanding. Anger and bitterness take hold.

The parents of those girls who were killed, along with their family members and neighbors, decided not to allow the shooting to separate them further from their neighbors. There were no lawsuits filed by the victims' families against the shooter's estate or the emergency services or the government, as is so often the case. They would not permit anger or fear to drive them into installing telephones or other modern conveniences that their way of life had survived so long without. They would trust God to protect them, leaving open the gates to their hearts and their communities, and move forward with forgiveness.

Given what happened, could that really be possible?

Amish buggy at dusk

CHAPTER TWO

Nickel Mines, Asleep

M IDNIGHT. OCTOBER 2, 2006. I was home sleeping, but having spent my lifetime in Lancaster and having driven those roads late at night, I know how bright the stars can be, how dark the shadows. Knowing the intersection of Mine Road and White Oak Road, I imagine it was quiet as usual. The unassuming convergence of these two roads—Mine Road running north and south, White Oak crossing it from east to west—forms the small town of Nickel Mines. The occasional milk truck making nightly rounds has little traffic to contend with, save for a raccoon or deer darting across the road. A large number of the households surrounding that small intersection are Amish, their farms and businesses tucked away in the hills and rolling valleys. But there are also many non-Amish (or English, as the Amish refer to us) who live in Nickel Mines. Still, with so many Amish in the area, night seems to come earlier, since fewer houses have electricity to power a television, or lights in every room.

During the day, Nickel Mines is a peaceful place: silos, trees, and row upon row of corn and tobacco define most of the horizon. The roads are barely wide enough for two cars to pass, and the electrical wires following alongside those narrow roads do not always follow the long driveways back to the farms—Amish farms do not need electricity, and the power lines pass them by. During that time of year, trees are shifting their colors from a late-summer green to shades of yellow and orange and red. Any corn still standing is drying out, the color of a scarecrow. The silos are tall, some already filled with a mixture of hay and corn for the winter months. The sky is large and inviting.

But at night all is quiet and dark: there is no glow of some distant city, and the streetlights can be counted on one hand. A stranger walking those back roads (some of them still lined with eight-foot-tall, unharvested cornstalks) might find the absolute quiet disconcerting. Any hint of a breeze will set those cornstalks to talking, their dried-out husks sliding against each other like a million pieces of brittle sandpaper.

Nickel Mines began its existence as a small mining town in the early 1700s, but it took over one hundred years for the mine to become a success, when in the 1850s a large vein of nickel was discovered. Soon after that, businessman Joseph Wharton, namesake of the renowned Wharton School of the University of Pennsylvania, combined the discovery of nickel with his own prestigious connections and convinced the government to go ahead with the "Shield" nickel, America's first five-cent piece that did not contain precious metals. The coin, engraved with a large shield on one side and the number 5 on the other side, was first minted in 1866.

During the height of its success, the nickel mine employed over 150 workers and in total mined 4.5 million pounds of nickel from as many as twelve separate shafts. In some years, Nickel Mines produced nearly 25 percent of the world's nickel, but by 1890 the mines were stripped, and mining came to an end in 1893. Those fertile, rolling hills quickly turned into farmers' fields.[1]

The Amish had begun settling in eastern Pennsylvania as early as 1736,[2] but history has little to say about the relationship between the Amish people and the mining village. One would assume they intermingled peaceably—in those days the Amish way of life was less visibly different than it is in the twenty-first century.

Yet in 2006 the intersection forming Nickel Mines remained, surrounded by many Amish, and the population would appear to have barely increased from the heyday of the nickel mines. Horses still pulled plows through the fields, and small Amish boys drove the teams as their fathers hefted the hay bales onto the wagons. The old church, Nickel Mines Mennonite Church, remained from the days of the mines, but most of the buildings at the crossroads had been added much more recently. Where the long farm lanes joined the main roads, small stands advertised baskets of produce or baked goods.

The Nickel Mines auction house was situated at the cross-roads. An aging roof covered the stucco exterior, surrounded by a large, mostly unpaved parking lot. There was usually a milk truck in the lot: some local driver who needed a place to park his rig after a long night of work. The auction house was quiet most of the week, except on Thursday evenings, when visitors came from all around in the hopes of finding a deal.

I went to the Nickel Mines Auction many years in search of spare tires or wheels for the automotive business I owned at the time. On that night I remember the building bustling and heaving with people, the convincing shouts of auctioneers, and the discreet, pensive nods of bidders. Hopeful people entered the building and passed by those on the way out, their arms full of purchases.

But just after midnight, as the October night drifted toward morning, the auction house would have held only silence; its windows dark, its doors locked, its parking lot empty.

A few hundred yards up White Oak from the auction house is a public swimming pool, home of the Nickel Mines Pool and Swim Club. To me it has always seemed out of place in the middle of all that farmland. In the summer months children swarm inside its chain-link fence like ants in brightly colored costumes, a strange contrast to the quiet, natural surroundings. A white three-rail fence surrounds the stone parking lot. Shouts ring out along with splashes, ice cream melts on children's faces, and cars pull in and out of the small parking lot on those hot midsummer days. But by October it is locked up and the pool is covered, a quiet slab of concrete surrounded by chain link topped with barbed wire in the middle of a Pennsylvania paradise.

The Nickel Mines Amish schoolhouse was located just across from the swimming pool on White Oak, and was one of many Amish schools within a ten-mile radius. The school, clearly viewed from the road, had side and back windows that offered views of open fields in every direction. With attendance hovering around twenty-six children, the school served Amish families within walking distance. A stone lane, maybe fifty yards long, led through a gated fence onto the acre or so of land and up to the small, block building painted yellow. A few of the windows had yellow "Have a Happy Day" smiley-face stickers on them. The lane stopped directly in front of a covered porch that stretched the entire width of the school. Two outhouses (approximately fifteen yards to the right of the building as you faced the front door) served as restrooms for the children. Flanked by only a few large trees and recently harvested cornfields, the small schoolhouse blended in well with the serene backdrop.

Just after midnight everything would have been dark and quiet as usual. The only difference I recall from that night was that the air felt unseasonably warm for October. Insects chirped. Walking by a barn, you may have heard the rustling of cattle or seen the glowing eyes of a tabby cat on the prowl for field mice. Like the dozens of villages settled on other crossroads in the valley, Nickel Mines was as bucolic and peaceful a place as you could find in America.

Thirty-two-year-old Charles Roberts made his way back from the last pickup of the day. It was just after midnight—the stars were sharp in the dark sky that night. He pulled his milk truck into his employer's parking lot and began emptying its contents. He was determined to do what he had planned. The letters were already written. The equipment was already stored away in the shed beside his house. The list that was tucked away in his glove compartment itemized the things he still needed to buy in the morning before he carried out his plan.

I did not know Charles Roberts personally, but I know his friends called him Charlie. Born December 7, 1973, in Lancaster County, Pennsylvania, Charles Carl Roberts IV's childhood apparently was as normal and unremarkable as that of any other youngster who grew up in the area. His father was a policeman and his mother homeschooled him, which was not all that unusual in this region. They lived in the country, surrounded by fields and forests. There would seem to be nothing out of the ordinary in his youth that could explain his actions of October 2, 2006.

Charles became interested in carpentry while his parents were building a house, and eventually got a job working on a framing crew, putting together the bare-bones skeletons of homes. In 1996 he quit construction for a less seasonal job: installing residential garage doors.

At the age of twenty-two Charles got engaged, and his fiancée finished out high school in the midst of preparations for a November wedding. By the end of 1996 everything in his life was looking positive—he was married and in love, both he and his wife had steady work, they had purchased a town house, and they were expecting their first child. Charles then turned his attention to becoming a truck driver—his in-laws had a trucking company, and he began practicing with his father-in-law in hopes of getting the Class A license required for driving tractor trailers.

But then came a turning point in Charlie's life. On a cold day in November his daughter was born prematurely and died twenty minutes after birth. He took some time off work, and everyone could tell that he was devastated. The infant's heart-shaped gravestone was etched with the image of a lamb along with the following inscription:

ELISE VICTORIA
pledged to God
daughter of
Charles and Marie
born and died
November 14, 1997

In 1999 Charles reached his goal of becoming a truck driver and was hired by his in-laws' company. The lives of those milk-truck drivers can at times be lonely. The nighttime shifts allow for very little interaction with anyone else, and for many of the drivers the circuit can sometimes be one constant battle to keep their eyes open. Pulling up to a milk tank, connecting the truck, filling up, driving off . . . and repeat, time and time again, until the wee hours of the morning.

Before the Amish had access to telephones, milk-truck drivers would often be the ones to pass important information from one farm to another: a recent birth or death, or important happenings within the community. Even though the Amish get by without modern conveniences, they still sell their milk the same way a dairy farmer would, with large tankers coming in to haul away their product.

In more recent years the milk-truck drivers have probably not been quite as known for being the conveyors of news they once were, yet they often will still spend time chatting with the farmers, and many of the Amish get to know their milk-truck drivers very well. Charles, however, had a reputation for keeping to himself.

Early the morning of October 2, Charles, at the end of a typically long shift, emptied his tank—up to fifty thousand pounds of raw milk. As I reflect on the event that would change the lives in my community forever, I can't help but wonder if he knew this would be his last milk delivery.

One of his fellow milkmen spoke through the morning's darkness.

"See you later, Charlie."

"Yeah, I'll see ya."

Charles didn't make any move to hang around and talk. The coworker wasn't surprised, though, and turned back to complete his own tasks—that was Charlie. During the weeks leading up to the shooting, people who knew him say he became more outgoing and talkative, something the police explained often happens after someone has made a final decision to go through with a crime. But in those last days he had become more withdrawn again, keeping to himself, rarely talking.

Charles left the dairy and drove through the dark night to the

Nickel Mine Auction, where he dropped off the milk truck and drove his own vehicle home, a drive that took only a few minutes. When Charles slid into bed that morning, around 3 a.m., he fell asleep quickly. His wife, used to the late-night routines of her husband, barely stirred.

Charles, we know from those who were close to him, was not a contented man, and at the heart of his burning discontent was the death of his daughter, Elise Victoria, more than ten years before. The despair he carried from the day he bore her small coffin from Georgetown United Methodist Church to the cemetery shaped his life forever. Something precious had been taken from him, and the initial anger that often comes with tragedy consumed him. Was he about to try to even the score? We will never know, yet there in his house, early that morning, he slept, as did many others whose lives would change that day. Firemen slept peacefully, unaware that it might be the last peaceful night's sleep they would have for years. Ambulance drivers and volunteer workers rested, less than twenty-four hours away from a horrifying scene that would plague their minds indefinitely. Amish families slept. Even if they had bad dreams, nothing could compare to the nightmare they would face when the sun rose.[3]

Nickel Mines Schoolhouse nestled in a peaceful pasture

CHAPTER THREE

Converging on an Amish School

SOMETIMES IT IS difficult for us, in this modern era, to understand how much noise and static we live with—the constant sound of traffic, the radio playing, the voices on the television shouting at us from some corner of the house, MP3 players and advertisements bombarding our senses. Our cell phones rarely leave us, and at any time their ringing steals us from whatever moment we are in.

Contrast this with the typical Amish household. There are no phones in the house. The few families who have decided to have a phone build what I call "phone shanties"—outhouselike sheds halfway up the drive to keep this modern device out of their homes. There are no electrical appliances in the house, so no constantly humming air conditioner or tumbling dryer or beeping microwave. No televisions or radios, of course. The sounds you hear inside an Amish home all have a pleasantness about them: a breeze blowing through open windows, songbirds singing in the trees, cows bellowing as they line up to enter the milk parlor, and horses stomping their steel shoes impatiently on the concrete barn floor. Perhaps most pleasant of all is the sound of children's voices, whether at play or working alongside their parents.

Visitors to Lancaster County always ask us questions about the Amish, the most prevalent being: How do they make it financially? What in the world do kids do without video games or television? The Amish life of simplicity should never be confused with poverty or boredom. While it is true that the Amish generally do not attend school much past the eighth grade and therefore do not pursue high-paying careers, they are industrious and remarkably wise about money. They learn early on to be resourceful with their hands, excelling at construction and other skilled work such as furniture making and, of course, farming. Amish women are legendary for their quilts and other handcrafted items and also sell their delicious baked goods and homegrown fruits and vegetables. Children learn these skills from their parents and often join in on the work at an early age. It's not unusual for all family members over the age of fourteen to be earning money with their skills, but what *is* unusual is their discipline in saving the money they earn. Coupled with the fact that they don't have utility bills, car payments, or credit card debt, it's easy to understand why many Amish families are actually quite well-off financially.

When it comes to Amish kids living without television, all you would need to do is spend a day in an Amish home and you'd have your answer: Amish kids seem to be not only content with their simpler lives, they actually appear to have more fun than their English counterparts. Part of this has to do with how the Amish live in general. The mornings begin before the sun comes up and are filled with chores: tending to the animals and the garden and preparing the house for the day. Everyone helps in this process, and everyone, even the children, seem to understand their importance in maintaining a well-run household. "Work" for these Amish children consists of climbing up into hay mows, bottle-feeding baby sheep and calves, or rolling out pie dough.

During the day, the younger children head off to school, often meeting up with friends on the network of paths leading to the schoolhouse. The Amish schools, when compared with ours, present a stark alternative that helps explain why Amish kids tend to enjoy school more than typical American students. Our schools are sprawling campuses to which students are shipped from miles away, often resulting in a half-hour ride on a noisy, often unruly bus. Public schools must work hard in order to create a community connection among the students, since most of them live so far apart from one another. The teachers are often strangers to the area, in many cases living in towns or cities far away from the school.

Contrast that with Amish schools, normally one-room buildings with a school bell, a few outhouses, maybe a water pump, and a three-rail fence around the one-acre property. There are no televisions or computers. Usually, the total number of students in the school is somewhere between fifteen and thirty, all of them living within walking distance of the school and one another. Every fall, winter, and spring I will see these children making the trek to their school, some riding small scooters on the roads, others choosing to cross the fields, the most direct route. Because they walk to school, the Amish keep the walking distance down to a mile or two by building several schools in a relatively small area and placing them close to clusters of Amish farms and homes.

Unlike public school students, Amish kids never have to worry about keeping up with current fashions. The boys wear straw hats with black bands, black trousers, and solid-colored shirts with black suspenders. The girls wear long, plain dresses, their hair up in a tight bun, covered with a handkerchief or a covering. In the summertime, the children might run barefoot to school, even through the fields. You will usually find them traveling in family units, brothers and sisters walking together, the older ones helping the younger ones along. There's no need to get to know one another on the first day of school, since everyone already knows everyone else.

Their teachers are generally young—sometimes barely out of their teens—and largely self-taught beyond their own eighth-grade schooling, but in terms of the basics of reading, math, history, and science, the Amish are very well educated. Also, the Amish may be the world's greatest users of public libraries. When we built the Family Center of Gap, we included space for a branch of the area's public library because we knew what a treasured resource it was to the Amish. Typically, an Amish mom will visit the library with her children, carrying a large basket. When they leave, there could be as many as twenty books in the basket, and in less than a week the family will be back, repeating the process. And it's not just children's books that they check out. Although their formal education ends at the eighth grade, many Amish are lifelong learners.

While the younger children are in school, the older children either work alongside their parents to help them earn a living or get jobs of their own, such as working on an Amish construction crew. Even the grandparents pitch in to do what they can to help out. At home, the families speak mostly Pennsylvania Dutch, a German dialect, but they also learn English at an early age.

The presence of the older generation is not simply endured—it is appreciated, nurtured, and cherished. You will see many an Amish farmhouse with what looks like multiple additions built on to the side of the house—these are built by the parents for their own parents to live in. They know that someday their parents will pass on, and then they will move in to the addition and their children will take over the house.

The Amish pay frequent visits to relatives or friends who live close by. They walk or pack everyone into the horse and buggy, and a trip that takes us ten minutes might take them an hour. Imagine traveling with our families at that kind of pace, without the interruption of cell phones or the noise of radios or DVD players.

The Amish tend to work around the natural hours of sunlight. The evenings are usually quiet affairs, with dinner together as a family, then peaceful time spent reading or quilting. If the children aren't reading, they're either playing table games like Monopoly or Rook or outside playing Bag Tag or Prisoner's Base. Perhaps one more round of chores needs to be done, and then the day is over.

•

FOR THE Miller family, the morning of October 2 began like any other morning in Nickel Mines. Held in their shared oak bed like two caterpillars squeezed into a single cocoon, sisters Lena and Mary Liz Miller slept the peaceful sleep of innocence. Their breathing came and went, soft and deep, their blue eyes lightly closed. Their dolls lay quietly in their own beds, tightly tucked in. The handmade quilt covering the sisters rose and fell in a gentle rhythm, its tight stitches evidence of an accomplished quilter.

Sometimes, if they moved close together while they slept, the difference in their hair color became more evident: eight-year-old Mary Liz's hair was dark, while seven-year-old Lena's was a lighter shade of brown. Even for sisters, they were close: they shared a room, shared a bed, and spent nearly every waking moment together. Only a year apart in age, they could not remember a moment in their lives when the other wasn't present.

As the sun was rising—not yet showing itself but lighting the sky from a dark black to a deep plum and finally to a whitish blue—the house stirred. Mary Liz and Lena, their little sister, and their two little brothers could all sense the day approaching their farmhouse and the surrounding barns. There were five children in that house, each one eight years of age or younger: a cozy, happy home.

Soon the sisters were awake and yawning, putting on their dresses, rubbing their eyes. The morning went quickly as the children helped with chores around the house, ate their breakfast, and prepared for school. Before the girls knew it they were out the door, carrying their brand-new lunch boxes, and passing a neighbor's house. Normally this neighbor would see the girls on their way to school, sometimes calling out a hello as they passed, but on that morning the neighbor didn't look outside. The girls' small feet passed by, unnoticed.

Across the way, Rachel Ann Stoltzfus woke up. Her four older brothers, two younger brothers, and one younger sister were busy with their morning chores. A fourth grader, she quickly dressed for school, ate breakfast, helped with the dishes, then rushed out the door with her three school-age brothers, Rachel holding tight to her purple Igloo lunch box. On that particular morning, her parents would later recall, there were no kisses good-bye.

Two more girls, the only sisters in a family with six brothers, also prepared to leave for school: Sarah Ann and Anna Mae Stoltzfus (although many Amish share the same last name, it does not necessarily mean they are related). Both girls were tall for their age, loved to jump on the trampoline in their yard, and were hard workers. They each had a small bowl on their dresser where they would leave lighthearted notes for each other, jokes, or silly things they thought to write.

Eight-year-old Sarah Ann loved to read, something that opened up a whole new world for her, and she had her nose in a book as often as possible considering the busy atmosphere of the house. Twelve-year-old Anna Mae was the numbers girl and worked the cash register for her parents at their farmer's market stand. Both girls loved their roles in the family, so much so, in fact, that on that morning, Anna Mae didn't want to leave until she had finished the laundry. In spite of her protests, the rest of the family bustled her out the door. They said they would finish it for her—she mustn't be late.

So she hurried off, catching up with her sister, brothers, and other classmates walking to school. Already the sun felt rather warm for an October day, and the air smelled more of summer fields than it did of falling autumn leaves.

While most Amish kids looked forward to school, one young girl in another home did not. For some reason, Naomi Rose Ebersole always hated leaving her family to go to school. On that morning, when it came time for her to walk to school, she fought back tears as she often did, her big, dark eyes filling to the brim. Her parents consoled her, reminding her that once she got to school the day would go by quickly. The second grade couldn't wait, and soon Naomi found herself walking to school through a small strip of trees with two of her brothers. She had three other brothers who had since completed their schooling. Soon she could see the school—her friends would be there waiting for her. She knew that once the lessons started the time would pass quickly, just as her parents had told her, and then she could return home, shout to her mother that she was back, and maybe even convince one of her brothers to play dolls, as they occasionally did to humor her. After all, she was the only little girl in the family.

Naomi was often heard humming her new favorite hymn:

My heavenly home is bright and fair
I feel like traveling on
No pain nor death can enter there
I feel like traveling on.[1]

In yet another farmhouse just west of the school, six-year-old Rosanna King snapped awake, taking only a moment to gather her senses before jumping out of bed. She loved mornings, loved waking up to a new day, and loved this new thing called school. It was her first year, and she was proving to be a good student even at such a young age.

After her morning routine, she and one of her two brothers ran down the lane where they would sometimes meet up with their friend Esther Rose. Esther was the second oldest girl in the school, and the younger ones looked up to her. A small girl for her age, with glasses, soft brown eyes, and brown hair, Esther knew what it was like to lose someone close—her father had died five years before when a car ran into his horse and buggy. She had two sisters and four brothers, and one of her brothers had been injured in the accident.

The five children often met at the end of the lane and walked toward the school together. The boys would run ahead while Esther and Rosanna walked behind, enjoying the beautiful morning.

Cutting through those autumn fields were three more girls, the Fisher sisters, the last of the eleven girls in that small school: Marian, who at thirteen was the oldest girl in the school and had her own room at home; Barbie, eleven; and Emma, nine, who was usually singing. The three girls also had one older brother and three younger brothers, one of whom joined them on the daily walks to school.

They were walking away from a home that contained four families and included their great-grandmother, their father's parents, and a widowed aunt with two children. For them, and for all the children on their way to school that morning, family was everything. Family and community. Most Amish in that area rarely travel far from Nickel Mines, except for those who operate farmer's market stands or go on vacation. They attend church and school and weddings and funerals together, and have for generations.

Sometimes Marian, Barbie, and Emma, along with their younger brother, joined up with the Stoltzfus sisters, Sarah Ann and Anna Mae. Chattering happily about normal, daily events, they would walk toward the school. But on that morning a neighbor saw only Anna Mae and Sarah Ann skipping through the field, arms swinging lunch boxes, dresses dancing. Perhaps Anna Mae still felt somewhat guilty about not having finished the laundry. Maybe eight-year-old Sarah Ann thought about the book she was reading, wondering what would happen next.

From the sky you would have seen them converging on the schoolhouse like tiny rag dolls bouncing toward a gleaming white dollhouse, the morning sun casting shadows and warming the autumn air. These Amish children—the boys in their suspenders and straw hats, the girls in their dresses and hair tied back in tight buns—were a picture from another era, some skipping, some walking slowly. They came from all directions that morning, cutting through the fields or walking the backcountry roads. As they approached the boundary of their schoolhouse, some of them climbed over the fence and some squeezed between the rails, while others, approaching from the road, came through the wide-open front gate.

A small sign just inside the schoolhouse offered this welcome in Pennsylvania Dutch: "Visitors brighten our day."

Amish windmill

CHAPTER FOUR

Point of No Return

JUST OVER FOUR hours after he went to bed, Charles Roberts woke up. The day had finally arrived. We will never know how he felt as the sun rose, whether or not any doubt crept into his mind about his plan. He woke up just after seven thirty that morning and helped his wife get their two oldest children ready for school.

Charles pulled on some jeans, a T-shirt, and a button-down shirt. A baseball cap covered his short brown hair. At six-two and two hundred pounds, he was a big man. His face had a soft look to it, almost boyish.

On the surface, the morning went along in the usual fashion

as the family prepared for the day. Charles rubbed the sleep from his eyes, helped feed the kids and get them out the door. About an hour later he was helping them onto the bus.

Then a strange thing happened: Charles called his children back off the bus. He squatted down beside them as they came down the bus's high steps. They probably wondered what was wrong, because he had never done that before. But he just hugged them again, straightened their clothes, mussed their hair.

"I love you," he said before ushering them back onto the bus.

The bus pulled away, heavy and slow, into the bright morning.

Back at the house, Charles's wife, Marie, didn't see the strange farewell—she was just trying to get out the door to her usual Monday morning prayer meeting. Another quick good-bye, another "I love you." Then she left, assuming her husband would be leaving soon for the drug test he had to take on a regular basis for his job. He was not a drug user, but the test was required to keep his commercial driver's license. It would be the first test he ever missed.

The morning was just beginning to burst in all its fall splendor as the sun shone over the surrounding trees and fields. If there was ever a time that Charles would have reconsidered his plans for that day, and evidence points to at least one such time, surely this would have been one. His children were safely off to school and he had just looked into their faces and told them he loved them. The routine beginnings of another week—many a Sunday evening plan has melted away in the mundane progressions of a

Monday morning. Even though he had carefully planned what he was about to do, he had yet to commit a crime. He could return the lumber and other supplies he had bought to help him carry out his plan, and everything would be fine.

But he did not change his mind. No one is sure exactly when he wrote the notes to his family that were found later. Perhaps he went back into his house and wrote them after Marie and the kids had left. The writing was in a slanting cursive, with a few words scribbled out and certain letters blacker than others from corrections. But for those who would later try to understand why he would do what he did, this note offered a clue:

> *I don't know how you put up with me all those years.*
> *I am not worthy of you, you are the perfect wife you*
> *deserve so much better. We had so many good memories*
> *together as well as the tragedy with Elise. It changed my*
> *life forever I haven't been the same since it affected me in*
> *a way I never felt possible. I am filled with so much hate,*
> *hate toward myself, hate towards God, and unimaginable*
> *emptiness it seems like every time we do something fun*
> *I think about how Elise wasn't here to share it with us*
> *and I go right back to anger.*[1]

Very few who came in contact with Charles would have had the first impression that he was angry or bitter. While he occasionally exhibited a quick temper, he did not appear to be a hateful man. Yet in his note to his wife it was this deep-seated frustration, hate, and regret, apparently kept hidden for all these years, that rose to the surface.

After the shooting, Marie described Charles as a loving husband and father in a statement released to the press:

> The man that did this today was not the Charlie I've been married to for almost ten years. My husband was loving, supportive, thoughtful, all the things you would always want, and more. He was an exceptional father, he took the kids to soccer practice and games, played ball in the back yard, took our seven-year-old daughter shopping. He never said no when I asked him to change a diaper. Our hearts are broken, our lives are shattered, and we grieve for the innocence and lives that were lost today. Above all, please pray.[2]

If Charlie *did* reconsider his plans, he quickly worked through his doubts and decided to continue. As soon as Marie left the house, Charlie went straight over to his neighbor's place to borrow his GMC pickup truck. He told the neighbor he needed to haul some lumber.

Once the truck was parked in his own driveway, Charlie began loading it with supplies he had purchased during the previous weeks from the local hardware store, Valley Hardware. It was the type of place where the employees knew or recognized just about every customer. The walls and shelves were lined with miscellaneous hardware items hanging on hooks or piled in bins: screws, hinges, tools, equipment. On a Tuesday in late September, only a week or so prior, Charlie had purchased two packages of thin plastic ties from Valley Hardware. A young Amish girl had helped him with his purchase. Two days later he would buy a stun gun from a local gun shop for thirty-five dollars.

He had hidden everything in a small storage shed attached to his house. On the morning of October 2, after Marie left the house, he packed those items into the covered bed of the borrowed pickup and proceeded to Valley Hardware for one final visit and a few last-minute purchases. Driving along the tree-lined streets and looking out over the fields, he must have reviewed the plan in his mind again and again.

Finally, after two separate purchases at 9:14 and 9:16 a.m., Charlie seemed to have all the items he wanted packed away in the truck: two-by-four and two-by-six wood planks, some with eye bolts already screwed into them; and four bags of plastic ties, tape, tools, nails, binoculars, batteries, flashlights, and a candle. He also carried a 9mm handgun, a 12-gauge shotgun, a .30-06 bolt-action rifle, and nearly six hundred rounds of ammunition. Clearly, Charlie was prepared to last this one out to the end.

One last item was packed away among the weapons and the hardware, an item that revealed the depths to which Charlie's mind had sunk: a tube of sexual lubricant.

A checklist, later found in a small spiral notebook hidden inside the cab of his milk truck, detailed each of the items Charlie had with him in the pickup truck that day. The list was compiled methodically, thoroughly, in an attempt to cover every possible eventuality. He drove the short distance back to the intersection of Mine and White Oak roads, parked the truck alongside the auction house, and waited.

THE SOUNDS of laughter bubbled up out of that one-acre plot as the children enjoyed their morning recess. Some of the girls sat together, talking, while others skipped around the yard. The younger boys ran, their energy bursting out of them like rays of light. The morning was gorgeous: the sun shown from a clear blue sky, and it felt like late spring.

There were visitors at the school that day—the teacher's mother and a few other mothers, some with young children. This wasn't unusual. Mothers and other relatives often visited the schools, helping children with their lessons and providing support for the teachers. As usual, the students would have been on their best behavior that morning with other adults in attendance.

From a distance, the scene looked perfectly idyllic, a moment in time from a past long gone, when children—the girls in dresses and the boys in straw hats—played outside in the sun and the grass and the dirt. There were no televisions for the children to stare mindlessly at, no computers around which their lives would center. It was a snapshot of fifty years ago. But it wasn't fifty years ago. It was October 2, 2006. And as all recesses do, that one went a little too fast. Soon it was time to go back inside.

As the children filed back into the school, Charlie, sitting in the truck at the intersection, watched from a distance, peering down White Oak Road through the trees. He could see the school yard and the two white outhouses. A white wooden fence made its way around the square property. The front gate, as usual, was open.

Then he saw what he was waiting for—the children began gathering together and making their way back into the school. Charlie pulled onto White Oak Road. He passed the local swimming pool on his left, closed now for over a month, waiting for next year's summer to come. He was barely on the road long enough to pick up speed before stopping just past the school lane. Turning the truck slowly, he backed all the way in, until his truck stopped at the front porch.

As he approached the schoolhouse, the gravel crunched under his tires. Less than a year later, when the new school would be built on a different property, it too had a stone driveway, as most of the schools have dirt or stone driveways. But after only a few days in the new school, the surviving children couldn't bear the sound of a vehicle driving over the stones. It reminded them too much of the day when Charlie's truck backed into their lane. And so the school board decided to pave the lane.

After shutting off the engine, Charlie walked up onto the front porch of the school, then stepped through the door. As he entered the schoolhouse, several heads turned to see who this visitor might be. Some of the children recognized the tall man as the driver of the truck that picked up the milk from their parents' farms. They didn't know his name. Perhaps knowing that the Amish are always quick to lend a hand, he asked the teacher if the students could help him find something. He spoke quietly. It was difficult for some to hear him. The teacher said they could help.

As he walked back out to his truck, he must have realized this was the point of no return. His truck was poised for a quick escape from the horrible path he was about to travel. Looking through the cab of the truck to the empty lane ahead, did he have second thoughts? I wonder. He could have driven away and no one would have thought twice. Or at the very least the teacher would have had a story to tell her family, about the milk-truck driver who randomly stopped by her school that day and acted strangely.

He reached into the truck and pulled out one of his guns and loaded it before walking back inside.

One of the boys would later recall hearing that sound. He was a hunter and knew the implications of that certain clicking. But by then it was too late. The man who hauled milk from their parents' farms was coming through the door, waving his gun as he issued his first set of instructions.

"Everybody to the front of the room. And get down!"

Amish child's shoes

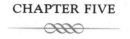

CHAPTER FIVE

"Shoot Me First"

A SUDDEN HUSH fell over the schoolroom. Some of the children looked at one another, trying to decide what was happening. Was this some sort of joke? Others couldn't stop looking at the small steel handgun in Charlie's hand; it looked so foreign to them. Then, as a group, they slowly stood. Chair legs scraped the floor. Some of the desks rumbled and bumped as the children quickly rushed to the front of the room.

The nightmare had begun.

As soon as Emma, the teacher, saw the handgun, she quickly slipped out the side door in one soft motion, hoping the gunman hadn't seen her leave. She felt her students would be okay with all the extra visitors in the schoolhouse. One of them, Emma Mae's mother, followed her out the door. Only a few weeks before, the teacher had had a quick discussion with someone regarding what to do in the case of an emergency—of course, they were talking more about what to do if someone fell on the playground and broke an arm, or needed medical attention. They decided at the time that Emma would run across the field to use the phone at one of the neighboring farms with a phone shanty. They could not have known the timeliness of such a plan.

"Somebody better go get her, or there's going to be shooting," Charlie said.

One of the younger boys said he would do it and ran out the side door and never looked back. I can imagine that little boy running across the field with the strength that fear infuses little legs and tender muscles. His lungs burned and his legs pumped faster than they ever had, but he couldn't catch his teacher or Emma Mae's mother until he arrived at the farmhouse.

Meanwhile, back inside, Charlie watched as everyone else made their way to the front of the room, by the blackboard. Some sat on the floor, some stood, waiting. What was this man doing? Why did he have a gun? Then he ordered the girls to lie on their stomachs.

"I won't hurt anyone if you just listen to me."

The eleven girls arranged themselves in a group along the front of the classroom and got down on the hard floor, their heads toward the chalkboard, looking over their shoulders to see what was going on. Always modest even at their ages, they made sure their dresses stayed pulled down to cover their legs. Charlie took the plastic ties and moved from girl to girl—with some of them he tied their hands and feet, and with others he tied them to one another. Anna Mae, who had wanted to finish the laundry, was not tied at all. There didn't seem to be any order to it. Already his plot was breaking down. He hadn't planned on anyone getting out. He hadn't planned on anyone going for help so quickly.

Scattered along the walls of the classroom, the boys sat with the guests who had come that morning. A strange quiet held the room. Charlie didn't say much. The women didn't talk. A little boy looked to one of the women for answers. He didn't say a word, but his eyes looked confused. The woman remained quiet, tried to look peaceful, and put her hands together in prayer. Silently the message spread through the room. Do not speak. Pray.

Mary Liz and Lena, the sisters who shared a bed at home, looked to one of the women sitting close by for answers. Lena asked her what this man was going to do and looked like she might begin to cry. "Cry quietly," the woman whispered, trying not to get Charles's attention.

"He won't hurt you if you listen to him," she said, looking deep into Lena's eyes. She believed Charlie when he had said that, believed that this tall, quiet man would not hurt her or the children. Why would he? He seemed too awkward and unimposing to do anything to them. Besides, these were children. Who could possibly harm a child?

But surely the gun eroded her confidence that everything would be all right. If it were only Charlie, things would seem much less intense, but the gun in his hand worried her.

Charlie stepped outside to bring in his supplies, leaving the door open as he strode to his truck. He reached into the bed and pulled out armloads of boards and tools. More ties. More weapons. Back and forth he went, forcing some of the boys to help him.

Naomi Rose, the second grader who didn't like going to school, couldn't keep from crying. Have you ever seen a seven-year-old girl trying not to cry? Her mouth was quivering, and large tears welled up in her dark eyes. One of the visiting mothers, heavily pregnant, tried to comfort her. Eventually, she lowered herself gingerly to the floor, lying beside the frightened girl. The woman would have her baby soon after the shooting. She would name the baby Naomi Rose.

At some point during this process, Charlie placed his handgun on a desk. One of the boys was close enough to see the shiny handle, the ominous barrel, and the trigger that could change everything. He wanted to grab it and run, make for the door and never look back. Yet he remembered Charlie saying that no one would get hurt. And what if he reached for the gun and Charlie caught him? Maybe that would just upset him. This brave little boy was so torn over what to do, but Charlie never strayed far enough from the gun and soon picked it back up. After all the girls had been tied up, Charlie told the women they were free to leave, and they could take their toddlers and babies. He could not have known the visitors would be there that morning, and I'm sure their presence disrupted his plan significantly.

The women didn't know what to do. *Listen, and no one will get hurt*, they remembered him saying. If they insisted on staying, it might set Charlie off. They walked out the door, but as they left they felt a strange sense of peace in that small building. One of the women later said she could sense God there with them, with the children. Two others said they saw an angel above the school.

"You boys can leave, too," Charlie said shortly after the women left with the babies, motioning his gun toward the side door.

At first they just looked at one another and at the girls tied up at the front of the room. The older boys didn't feel right leaving. They wanted to stay. They wanted to protect the girls. But what can a twelve-year-old boy do in the face of an unstable man with a handgun? Reluctantly, they left. But once outside, they just scuffled about like lost children. They didn't know where to go or what to do. Some of them still had sisters inside the building and didn't want to leave. Soon they found themselves huddled behind the outhouses, a group of boys in black suspenders and straw hats, praying like they had never prayed before, wishing there were something they could do to help the girls in their schoolhouse.

Inside, Charlie began preparing the room. The first step was to lower the shades, so he made his way around the room to each of the windows, pulling down the blinds. One of them spun back up, all the way to the top, so Charlie pulled a desk over; he clambered on top of it so he could reach the top of the blind, clumsily clinging to his handgun. He wanted to block out any view into the school. Preoccupied with the blinds, he didn't see one of the girls move toward the door.

Emma, whose older sisters, Marian and Barbie, were at the

front of the room with her, heard the slightest whisper of a voice speak soft instructions.

"Now would be a good time to run."

A fraction of a moment passed, Charlie still fumbling with the blind, then climbing down from on top of the desk and turning around. But Emma, whose feet had not been bound, was gone, barely breathing as her feet darted across a dusty field, leaving more and more distance between her and that small school on White Oak Road.

Later, Emma would say she thought one of the women told her to run, but none of the women issued such an instruction. An angel, perhaps? Or maybe a suggestion from one of the girls who wouldn't make it out of that small schoolhouse alive? Emma's survival would be seen as one of the many miracles that took place that day.

If Charlie had realized that a girl had escaped, he didn't mention it. He continued barricading the room, which now held the final ten girls. Desks were pushed up against the doors. Two-by-fours were nailed in place, blocking off windows and further reinforcing the doors, darkening the room. Charlie had worked in construction, and the hammer moved quickly and efficiently in his hands. The nails slid skillfully into place. He fastened plastic ties around the door handles. Soon the room was completely sealed from the outside world. No one could come in or get out easily.

It was then that Charlie heard the girls praying. Their eyes were closed and their voices were quiet, but I am sure there was a fervent resolve in those prayers. They must have prayed the way people do when they find themselves in a hopeless situation: begging to be spared, desperate for deliverance.

Charlie had attended church, and his wife was a devout Christian. He obviously knew what they were doing. It's safe to assume that, with his upbringing and the time he spent in church, he believed in heaven and hell. Maybe that's why he asked a special request of the girls.

"Pray for me," Charlie muttered to the whispering girls as he nervously paced around the room, double- and triple-checking the boarded windows and tied doors.

"Why don't you pray for us?" one of the girls said to him, turning the tables, if only for a moment.

"I don't believe in praying," he said firmly, then turned to resume his preparations. The time had come for the first part of Charlie's plan: sexual assault.

"If just one of you will let me do what I want, I won't hurt the others," he promised.

Perhaps one of the older girls understood what Charlie was talking about, because one of them whispered quickly to the younger girls in Pennsylvania Dutch.

"Duh's net! Duh's net!" (Don't do it! Don't do it!)

When no one volunteered, Charlie walked forward and grabbed one of the girls by her legs. She kicked furiously at his hand. The tension that had been building in the room suddenly transformed into a desperate fear that things were about to start happening. Some of the girls screamed for help, others screamed at Charlie.

But then, just as quickly as he had walked to the front of the room and resolved to do the unspeakable, he stopped. He could hear the sound of cars driving up the gravel lane and parking not too far away. The atmosphere of the morning went from a terrified silence to urgent action. He dropped the girl's leg and ran to a door and peeked through one of the cracks.

The police were stationing themselves outside the schoolhouse, guns drawn. Charlie was running out of time.

Then came the one moment of wavering that could have changed the events of the day. For a few brief seconds, Charlie stood there in the barricaded schoolhouse and looked down at the ten girls lined up on the floor across the front of the room. The blinds were drawn, the doors nailed shut. He most likely knew that more policemen were now creeping around outside the building, looking for a way to rescue the girls. Police radios barked just twenty or thirty yards away.

He turned and took a few steps toward the front door, mumbling something about giving up. For that one short moment he may have considered walking out the door and into that beautiful fall day, hands in the air. Just walk away from it all. He knew he would have been shoved to the ground and handcuffed. He knew he would be in a lot of trouble, and there would be questions. He knew he would have all kinds of explaining to do, probably serve jail time or be forced to receive psychiatric examinations. But he could still back out. He could still be a father to his children, a husband to his loving wife.

Ten sets of innocent eyes watched him as he walked toward the door. They could feel how close it was to ending. Dare they hope that he would leave them? Some of them wanted to cry out for help.

Then Charlie stopped, shoulders hunched over. He turned around, away from the door and away from the girls' last shred of hope.

"I'm sorry," he mumbled. "I have to do this."

He took his cell phone out of his pocket. He called his wife's cell phone but didn't get an answer, so he left her a message. It scared her when she received it, something about what he was about to do and how sorry he was. She called the police, even though she didn't know where her husband had gone.

What had he actually planned to do in the first place? Had his initial expectation been to get into the school, sexually assault the girls, and then escape? If so, why did he barricade the doors and windows in a way that made a quick getaway nearly impossible? Had he only barricaded the doors and windows because someone had gone for help? Yet if he hadn't been planning on a long, drawn-out affair, why had he come to the schoolhouse so well equipped to board up the school and so heavily armed?

In any case, he had to get rid of them, those police setting up operations outside the schoolhouse. He needed some peace and quiet. His plan was falling to pieces. He called 911.

"I just took, uh, ten girls hostage and I want everybody off the property or, or else," he said.

"Okay," the emergency responder replied in a calm voice.

"Now!" he demanded.

"Sir, I want you to stay on the phone with me, okay? I'm going to get the state police down there on the phone. I need to let you talk to them, okay? Can I transfer you to them?"

"No, you tell them what I said and that's it. Right now or they're dead, in two seconds. Two seconds, that's it!"[1]

He hung up on the call center. He knew he couldn't back down now.

Charlie turned and looked at the girls, determination in his voice. There was a change in him at that moment. He was no longer the quiet Charlie who mumbled instructions when he first arrived. The hate and the anger that had smoldered inside of him for ten years began to rise, to burn out of control, to rage in all of its dreadful bitterness.

"I'm going to make you pay for my daughter," one of the girls recalled him saying in a firm voice.

OUTSIDE, AN Amish man stood leaning against the white fence, struggling to catch his breath. Police officers swarmed around the building, biding their time, keeping their distance, assuming that Charles Roberts would not hesitate to fire shots at anyone who left themselves in the open. A few other emergency vehicles were waiting off in the distance, but the Amish man wasn't worried about anything except the children inside the school. Seven of his relatives were there that morning, and, as far as he knew, only his daughter Emma, the teacher, had escaped. His friends and neighbors were gathering along the fence as well, as news had spread quickly from farm to farm, as neighbors alerted neighbors of the emergency at the schoolhouse.

About fifty years old, the Amish man wore a straw hat with a narrow black band. His work clothes were worn but well made. He wore black shoes, and his trousers had black suspenders that wrapped around his shoulders. A small pin, barely visible, in each of the suspenders held them in place. His eyes were kind, like the eyes of a grandfather, and his hands were cracked and calloused from years of hard work.

He could hear police officers shouting into their radios, begging their superiors to let them raid the school, but the same answer was repeated, "Wait, wait." No one knew how serious Charles Roberts was about shooting anyone—any quick motion on their part might scare him into doing something he wouldn't otherwise do. So they all waited.

Now that they had his cell number, the officers tried to reach Charles Roberts on his phone. Over and over they dialed. If they could only talk to him, or if one of his loved ones could have a word with him, maybe then he would change course. Come outside. Turn himself in.

INSIDE, THE girls waited, the older ones looking to one another for strength. Charlie walked toward the front of the room and that line of ten little girls, and as he approached, he raised one of the guns to his shoulder and pointed it.

"Shoot me first," thirteen-year-old Marian blurted out quickly, perhaps thinking of her younger sister Barbie, still in the room.

"Shoot me next," said her eleven-year-old sister, Barbie.

Gunshots rang out.

Charlie had listened. He shot Marian first.

THE AMISH father of the teacher heard shots in quick succession: *one, two, three* shotgun blasts, then *four, five, six* gunshots, and they continued. The police ran for the front door. A shotgun round blasted through the boarded window on the front door, shattering glass and splintering wood, implanting shards of shot in the windshield of the truck Charles Roberts had been driving, pushing the police back

The Amish man standing by the fence collapsed to his knees. All along the fence his neighbors, who had made their way to the school, stood in shock, then, like him, fell to their knees in prayer, or horror, holding the wooden rails for support. Certainly this was all a dream. Surely someone would shake them and they would rise up through that blue sky, beyond the clouds, and find their heads on pillows, the sun rising, the morning not yet begun.

Some of the policemen approaching the school ducked instinctively behind their shields, but they all kept moving toward the front door, then faster when the shots continued.

For an entire minute the police battered at every door and window trying to gain entrance, but the doors had been nailed together, the handles tied with plastic ties, the windows boarded over. Eventually the lead officer used his shield to smash in what remained of the window on the front door and, just before diving through, quickly told the officer behind him to be ready to take Charlie out. Fortunately for him, as he crashed through the window and into the school, the shooting had stopped.

Charles Roberts had already taken his own life with a single shot. He was dead on the scene. Around him lay ten girls, all shot and bleeding. The room was covered in blood and broken pieces of desks and glass. The smell of gunfire hung in the room, a dark, smoky, burning scent.

For those brief moments outside the school, the teacher's father couldn't move. He was on his knees beside the fence as the state troopers around the school rushed toward the door and then inside. Then, out of nowhere, as if in a dream or from a great distance, he heard a voice yelling his name with news he never thought he would hear.

"Your family is okay—they're over at the farm!"

He wanted to run straight to the farm, but, knowing his own family was safe, his concern immediately turned to those in the school. He slipped through the fence and walked toward the school. The police were still too concerned with the girls to take time blocking off access, so he made his way toward the scene without being stopped.

When he got to the front door of the school he didn't want to look inside. He knew he shouldn't look through that door. But he did—he quickly glanced into the shadows. And what he saw—the chaos, the bullet casings lying all over the floor, the blood everywhere—was something he wished he had never seen.

The officers quickly began carrying the girls from the school. Normally they wouldn't move victims so soon after an incident without performing first aid immediately, but the conditions inside the room made it impossible to do any work there. Due to the barred windows, there was no light. The desks were pushed here and there, debris covered everything, and there were ten girls needing treatment. The state policemen knew they would have to move the girls just so the paramedics could get to them. So they carried them outside, laid them gently on the ground. Many of them were talking to the girls, whispering words of encouragement.

"Hang in there."

"You can make it."

"We've got you now, you'll be okay." Some of them started tearing up their coats to make tourniquets in an attempt to stop the girls from bleeding to death.

By the end of it they would be covered in the girls' blood.

Emergency scene at the schoolhouse

CHAPTER SIX

My Heavenly Home
Is Bright and Fair

I T IS EASY to see how Gap, a small town in Lancaster County, got its name. It sits literally in the "gap" between two neighboring hills that spread gently down into a rolling valley covered with alfalfa and cornfields. It's only a few miles from where I grew up, and it's where the Family Resource and Counseling Center is located. Gap is also about five miles from Nickel Mines, and the two towns are separated by trees, more cornfields, and a few twisting backcountry lanes.

A large clock tower, built in 1892, stands at the gap between those two hills, looking down over the community. Time has done little to change this place: the people still know each other well, much as they did fifty years ago, and the Amish still drive through the streets in their horse and buggies, the sound of their clip-clopping hooves nearly as common as the sound of eighteen-wheelers with their Jake brakes screeching as they rumble to a stop at the bottom of Gap Hill.

The small town of a few thousand people is formed, as many small towns are, by the intersection of two major roads: U.S. 30, a highway running east and west, connecting Atlantic City, New Jersey, with Astoria, Oregon; and Route 41, which runs south to Wilmington, Delaware. Houses line both highways, and Gap sits mostly to the south of Route 30. Neither highway is very straight, and both have many hills and winding streams to cross before the roads even out closer to the larger cities.

On that particular October 2, one of the non-Amish volunteer firemen, Rob Beiler (no relation to me), sat quietly at his desk in a small office in Gap. Rob is built like a football player, tall and broad-shouldered, but his voice sometimes surprises people with just how relaxed it sounds. He could never be accused of wasting words—they come out in measured, even tones.

Monday morning promised to be the beginning of another busy week for Rob. He sat at his desk, surrounded by all the things one would expect to find in the office of an insurance agent: file folders, a stack of mail, various notes, and framed pictures of his family. Not just any salesman, though, Rob owned the successful business and sold insurance to a large portion of the community. But on the corner of his desk there was something not commonly found on the desk of an insurance agent: a police scanner.

Rob grew up carrying a pager on his belt. His father was a

volunteer fireman, serving as assistant chief of the Gap Fire Department for more than twenty years. In 1977, when Rob was fourteen years old, his father was the chairman of the first Gap Fire Company sale, a fund-raiser that has since become an annual event. Rob missed only one of those sales, when he was off at Bible college, and he makes it a habit to attend the two ham-and-oyster dinners held every year to raise money for the fire company. Having been raised around the fire hall, Rob grew up chasing sirens and joined the department as soon as he was old enough, in November 1977. If there was anything more natural to him than the instinct to help people, it would be difficult to pinpoint.

Both the Gap Fire Company and the neighboring Bart Fire Company are comprised entirely of volunteers, and 75 percent of the Bart Fire Company is Amish. Though both departments rely on volunteers, they are highly respected for their professionalism, and the Amish firefighters are among the best in the region. The Amish also play a huge part in the fund-raisers, and their community supports the fire halls extensively. When the Amish firefighters come in to help with the fire company's sale or the various other fund-raisers held at the fire halls, they bring their families along—their wives and children jump right in and help make every event a success.

Over the scanner that morning, Rob heard the Christiana Community Ambulance receive a call from dispatch regarding a frantic member of the Amish community. Christiana, another small town about five miles south of Gap on Route 41, provides ambulance services to many of the smaller towns in the area, such as Atglen, Parkesburg, and Gap. The voices scratched their way through the scanner, and Rob listened, the way he always did, with one ear on the scanner and the other attending to his insurance business. Initially, though, the call came in only as an emotional problem and nothing was mentioned about a shooter. Later, Rob would discover the reason for this classification: the initial caller sounded hysterical, and the dispatcher couldn't get any information from the caller, so they called an ambulance in order to get the call started. It would be easy for a dispatcher to think twice about passing on any information about a shooter at an Amish school. It was just too unbelievable.

But even as the bedlam of that morning began to unfold, as Charlie stood in the classroom telling the women to leave with their babies, the call drifted from Rob's mind in an instant—he had plenty of work to take care of at the office, and he didn't think that someone being a little upset would be enough to sound the alarm that called volunteers to the fire department. It was the same everywhere that morning: normal Monday activities carried on, and people went about their business having no idea that they were about to be changed forever by the atrocious acts of someone in their own community.

Christiana is another one of those small eastern Pennsylvania towns with a few quaint streets winding up and over and around the train tracks that dash straight through the hills. While Route 41 is a truckers' road—in 1997 a national study was conducted that called Route 41 the third deadliest highway in the United States—Christiana is an island of a town surrounded by farming country. If you follow the tree-lined streets of Christiana in October, they fade off into the hills of western Chester County, and you quickly find yourself lost in beautiful, winding forest roads surrounded alternately by sloping farmers' fields and forest-covered hills yielding gold and red leaves.

At Christiana's emergency response center, just off the highway, two emergency medical technicians stand by to respond with each ambulance when they are called out. On the morning of October 2, one of the EMTs on duty, Vietta Wood, sat in the station talking to her partner, Samantha Jackson. Their time in the station was mostly spent filling out paperwork from previous calls, doing station chores, or just hanging out and talking.

When the call came in that morning, the call center initially dispatched Vietta and Samantha to a farm in Nickel Mines for an emotional problem, the same call that Rob heard from behind the desk at his insurance agency. Neither of the EMTs thought too much about the call as they got their gear ready, climbed into the ambulance, and pulled out of the station, sirens blaring. They had received plenty of "emotional problem" calls in their time as EMTs, and there was no reason to think this one would be any different from the myriad emotional breakdowns or domestic situations they had run into before.

Vietta knew those roads well—like most Lancaster County residents, she had grown up there, still lived close to her parents, and spent time with friends she had known since childhood. She had seen a lot of tragedy during her years as an EMT, but those things did little to dim her brilliant smile or kind personality. Cruising down those old roads, her mind automatically reviewed procedures and protocol. The calls EMTs respond to run the entire spectrum, from stubbed toes to massive strokes, from simple cuts to serious car accidents. But no car crash or heart attack victim could have prepared Vietta for the things she would see that day.

Normally, after the initial call, the dispatch center would come back over the radio and give Vietta an update such as "there is a couple having a domestic dispute" or "there is a young boy having trouble breathing." But on that call they didn't receive any additional details. The scanner was quiet.

Then the initial lack of information was followed by some confusing instructions: they were not to proceed to the farm where the call had been made, but were to stage at the corner of White Oak Road and Mine Road by the Nickel Mines Auction. Rob Beiler would hear these instructions over his scanner and wonder at the strangeness of them, that an ambulance would be called to the scene and then be asked to wait at a staging area hundreds of yards away.

By the time the ambulance was approaching Nickel Mines Auction, Vietta heard a few other updates and slowly began to realize what was going on. Then the school came into view, and immediately she knew. The scene was chilling. The building, normally nestled peacefully in the middle of those fields, was surrounded by police cruisers, some in the driveway and others parked in the surrounding fields. The state troopers moved around the perimeter fence with guns drawn like soldiers trying to avoid a sniper.

Vietta noticed the families lining the fence, too, just outside the crime-scene tape. Some held their heads in their hands, some paced back and forth. Amish women, in their solid colored dresses and hair coverings, held both hands over their mouths. Others were restrained by the police from running inside to rescue their children. When Vietta parked her vehicle she could hear parents crying out for their kids. Could the children hear those voices from inside the school?

Vietta and Samantha were a Basic Life Support (BLS) unit, as opposed to the Advanced Life Support (ALS) units stationed at hospitals. In severe situations, ALS units typically start IVs and administer drugs at the scene. Yet at that time, so soon after the call, Vietta and Samantha were the only ambulance crew on site, along with a fire truck (from Bart Fire Station, only a mile up the road on the outskirts of Nickel Mines), and what they were about to encounter would stretch their training to its limits.

Still waiting in the ambulance, Vietta could see the troopers beginning to gather at the front door and around the windows, looking for a way to get inside the schoolhouse. She called 911 and spoke with Sky FlightCare out of Brandywine Hospital. Her husband worked there but was not on duty that day.

"You guys have to get a medic unit and a helicopter on standby right away! Get in the air but do *not* fly over the scene, or anywhere close. Just be ready."

As Vietta continued talking with her husband's supervisor about the scene, a staccato sound pierced the morning: *Pop, pop, pop.* Over and over again. The police raced for the school. Vietta's hands clenched the steering wheel. The supervisor on the other end of the line could hear the gunshots.

"What's going on out there?" the supervisor yelled.

Vietta was speechless. She wondered how many children

were still in the school. At that point she didn't know that some of them had been allowed to leave.

The gunshots also stirred the parents and relatives standing along the fence like a stick poked into a bees' nest—they went from anxious and worried to frantic and desperate. Again police had to keep some of them from storming through the fence and into the school yard. Some fell knees-first onto the hard corn-fields. Others leaned against the fence like marionettes with their strings cut.

Vietta watched as the policemen first smashed their way through the front door, then began removing whatever it was that had kept the doors from opening in the first place. Soon they were filing in and out of the building—many officers racing into the schoolhouse, and then carefully walking back out, each carrying what looked like a sack of grain, some draped over their shoulders, some held close to their chests. Ever so gently, each laid his precious burden down on the grass outside the school.

That's when the officers began frantically waving Vietta to the scene. She pulled up in her ambulance and saw them lying there, the ten sacks of grain now transformed into ten small bodies all in a row, and each had at least one state trooper by her side. Some of the troopers tore off their shirts and used them to try to staunch the flow of blood seeping from their young victims. Others placed their hands tightly on pressure points to lessen the bleeding. They were all covered in a slick, red wetness that added weight to their clothing. The last thing Vietta said, before jumping out of the ambulance and entering the scene, she shouted over the radio.

"Put five helicopters in the air, *now!*"

THE CHATTER continued on Rob Beiler's scanner, and soon he heard the ambulance call back to dispatch that they were waiting in Nickel Mines and not going to the scene. Strange, he thought to himself: the ambulances usually jump straight in. Rob resituated himself in his chair and rested his chin in his hand, listening closer to the calls and the information being relayed back and forth.

Suddenly the requests began escalating far out of proportion to anything he would have expected—Pennsylvania State Police were on the scene requesting backup, multiple ambulances, and medical helicopters. Backup and helicopters? Rob put down his pen and sat quietly in his chair, pensive, now listening intently as events began to unfold. When their neighboring fire company, Bart Fire Department, was called to the scene, the responder in him took over—it was in his blood to get his own fire apparatus and rescue vehicles ready as quickly as possible, just in case they got the call.

He stood from his chair, straightened some items on his desk, and walked out of his office toward the door.

"Something's going on down at the Nickel Mines school-house," he told his coworkers over his shoulder, concern etched in his voice. "I'm going to the fire station in case we get the call."

During Rob's two-minute drive to the fire department, his pager finally went off, and this time the buzzing filled him with a strange foreboding. It wasn't like any other call he had received—there was a mysteriousness to what was happening in Nickel Mines, and he found himself feeling tense, on edge.

He pulled into the fire hall parking lot in the middle of Gap, surrounded by rows of historic homes, the traditional kind with large, covered front porches and steep peaks. At the top of the hill a long-abandoned train track came to an end on top of tall trusses in midair, perhaps once the dumping point for some sort of rail-bound material. A gray stone church was just around the corner from the fire hall, empty on that Monday, and beside it a large graveyard.

Inside the firehouse, Rob changed into his gear and began preparing the truck while other volunteers arrived. Rob listened to the scanner but picked up precious little information—there was a strangeness to the calls, and uneasiness settled into the pit of his stomach; he still had no idea what was going on in Nickel Mines, or why such a vast array of emergency medical teams were being called to the scene. In fact, he still didn't know exactly where the scene was.

Rob rode in the officer's seat in the rescue truck—he and three others rotate as duty chief for a week at a time, and that was his week on. A total of seven men rode in the truck with Rob as they cruised out of Gap on Mine Road toward Nickel Mines, approximately five miles away. Pieces of information kept trickling through—then they heard something about a gunman at an Amish school. A gunman? In Nickel Mines? It didn't seem possible.

But when the medical helicopters started getting called in, Rob heard confirmation that it was an Amish school. The first school he pictured was not the one on White Oak Road—there are numerous Amish schoolhouses tucked away in those fields.

The one he pictured in his mind was on Wolfrock Road. This school sits up on a tree-covered hill, surrounded by shrubs and tucked away in the forest, only barely visible from the road. Little did he know that this school would not have been ideal for Charlie Roberts's plan—too many bushes hindered the view from the windows, and someone inside would have precious little knowledge of what was going on around the perimeter.

The fire truck made a hard left, and coming into view was the Amish schoolhouse on Wolfrock Road. Rob looked intently at the school, expecting to see state troopers or ambulances, but what he saw sent goose bumps down his arms: a row of young Amish boys in straw hats stood on the white wooden fence, their legs stiff against the rails, hands shielding their eyes as they peered across the fields and into the valley where the Nickel Mines school sat. They were trying to see what all the commotion was about.

Suddenly the school across from the Nickel Mines public pool flashed through his mind. They continued on toward that school, following Mine Road.

Rob's fire truck was the third vehicle on the scene—the Christiana ambulance had arrived first, followed by the Bart Fire Company. By this time the ambulance had backed up to the school, and police were rushing in and out the schoolhouse door. State troopers ran around the school like ants around a disturbed anthill. Rob stared at the cornfields and woods surrounding the schoolhouse—was the shooter still out there? Was he still waiting to pick more people off? He turned to the guys in his truck.

"No one gets out until I come back."

He hopped out the door and found a state policeman.

"Sir, I need to know, is the scene secure? Is the shooter still on the loose?"

"No," he said. "The shooter is deceased."

The shooter is deceased. Such a simple pronouncement. For Rob it meant that he could allow his men to proceed to the scene. For Charlie's wife it would mean her husband, the father of her children, was gone. For Charlie's parents it would mean the loss of a son. So many things glossed over in such a short, but necessary, sentence. *The shooter is deceased.*

"Okay, what do you want us to do?" Rob asked quickly.

"Send all your men up to help with EMS," the policeman yelled over his shoulder. The shooting had just taken place, and there was still only the initial ambulance on the scene, the ambulance that had been called to respond to an emotional problem, the ambulance occupied by Vietta and her partner, Samantha.

Rob mustered his men and they ran toward the school. At most, five minutes had passed since the police stormed the building. The pickup truck Charlie drove to the school still sat outside the door, its back window blown out by the last shotgun blast he had directed at the state troopers before turning the gun on himself.

Rob caught his breath as he saw the number of victims lying in the yard outside the school: ten children lined up, each with a state trooper at her side. What had happened here? He ordered his men to help however they could, directing the more medically trained to join up with the emergency response teams.

Samantha and Vietta split up and began working at a

steady, methodical pace, going from girl to girl, quickly checking vitals, performing triage. Two or three EMTs from the Bart Fire Company's QRS (Quick Response Service) jumped in and started helping as well. Although her training enabled Vietta to respond with technical precision, adrenaline raced through her body as she began checking blood pressure, putting pressure on wounds, and shouting instructions to anyone who would help. Some of the troopers still held the wounded girls, urging them to hold on.

Rob's team did their best to help, but as he surveyed the scene he felt the effort was too little, too late. There were so many wounds to cover, so many children to treat, so many decisions to make. The scene was chaotic—ten girls were shot, the shooter had shot himself, helicopters were on the way, and only four medics were on the scene. Troopers ran in and out of the school, still wielding shotguns. Broken glass and shredded wood and shotgun shot littered the floor. There was blood everywhere, on the walls and the floor. Innocent blood. Vietta forged ahead, doing what she could to prepare the girls for their trips to the hospitals and emergency centers in the area.

One of the girls died almost immediately: twelve-year-old Anna Mae, who had wanted to stay home to help with the laundry. She was one of the first girls that the teacher's father saw when he ran down to the school yard, moments after finding out that his family was safe. He was devastated when he saw Anna Mae, and he didn't think anyone else would make it out of that school alive.

Rob looked inside the school. Mixed in with the evidence of

violence were the symbols of childhood innocence: desks and chairs, the chalkboard with writing on it, books and papers and projects. Pencils and pens and paper, everything shredded from the shooting.

Soon ambulances screamed in along White Oak Road, pulling to a quick stop in the grass beside the public swimming pool. Emergency medical staff rushed as fast as they could to the school, weighed down by their fluorescent orange bags and pieces of equipment. The atmosphere around the school was electric, tense.

Don't look at their faces, Rob told himself. It was the one way he could sleep at night after pulling someone from the wreckage of a car or listening to someone screaming in pain. When a leg is caught in a car, he focused on disentangling the leg. If an arm was caught, he focused on helping to free the arm. Ignoring faces allowed him to work, to focus, to remain emotionally detached from the situation. He and his men circled the scene, helping where they could.

But the girls were all in critical condition, and, despite the critical care given minutes after the shooting, another girl passed away before she could be taken to the hospital: second-grader Naomi Rose Ebersole, who would sometimes cry because she didn't want to go to school, who only that morning had been humming her favorite hymn:

> My heavenly home is bright and fair
> I feel like traveling on

No pain nor death can enter there
I feel like traveling on

Rob felt the girls were slipping away much too quickly, and it seemed there was nothing they could do about it.

Half of Rob's crew continued helping the medical team while he led the other half outside the fence to set up four helicopter landing zones. As the realization of what was happening settled in even further, Rob forced himself to focus on the intricacies of the tasks at hand: setting up the cones to establish a makeshift landing zone, pacing off the yardage to give plenty of clearance for the four zones, making sure there were no overhead obstructions.

Two landing zones were in the pasture, two more on the Nickel Mines Pool side of the road. When the cones were set, Rob kept himself busy by parking the ambulances as they came in—drivers pulled up to the school and sprinted inside the fence with their crew. Rob would park their vehicles just across the street, always keeping one lane clear.

These firemen and EMTs were regular members of the community—insurance salesmen, farmers, roofers. Many were Amish. And sure, they often saw the bad side of life—they had to cut people from their cars after drunk-driving accidents and put out deadly fires—but on that morning it was different. The horror of those events ate at their insides as they did their jobs. Most of what they witnessed were accidents or mishaps. Not this—this was premeditated. They helped carry those little children to the ambulances. They had to explain to bystanders that the shooter had killed himself, that the children were being rushed to hospitals all over the state. And they had to do this in their own community while feeling horrified and stunned that an evil so potent had appeared seemingly out of nowhere.

The Amish people were coming from all directions, much as their children had that morning and along the same paths. Many had been there, outside the fence, before the shooting began, but now there were even more of them, walking, even running, through the fields toward the school as news spread about the shooting. Rob had seen this many times before, at fires or accidents. The Amish just came. They wanted to help, and if there was nothing they could do to help, they wanted to offer support with their presence. Rob remembered an accident in which the driver of a car had struck an Amish buggy and killed the Amish man driving it. The accident was very close to the lane that led to the Amish man's house. Less than an hour after the accident Rob saw some of the Amish neighbors sweeping the lane clean and tidying up. When he asked them what they were doing they explained that the Amish community would come visiting soon and they wanted to help the family prepare the house. When something tragic happens, they come together.

Standing there, inside the white fence at the schoolhouse, Rob saw an Amish couple pleading with one of the troopers to let them into the school, and as Rob walked closer he overheard the policeman explain above their desperate voices that it was a crime scene. They couldn't cross the tape.

"My daughter's in there!" cried the man, his voice breaking, his wife literally hanging on to his arm. The blood drained from Rob's face as he thought of his own three children, how he would be feeling, how desperate he would be to get into the building. He wasn't sure if he would be able to accept a strange man telling him that he wasn't allowed into the school if his children had been in there.

"I'm sorry," the policeman said again, firmly. "You can't cross the tape."

The couple fell to their knees in unison, weeping, holding each other. Rob walked over and put his trembling hand on one of their shoulders.

"We're doing everything we can," he said softly, his voice cracking, a dull ache lingering in his throat. The words felt out of place and almost weak, but he felt he had to say something or try to comfort them somehow. Rob never found out whose parents they were or if they ever saw their child alive again.

Almost shell-shocked from the emotions, Rob turned to focus on landing the helicopters that would be arriving any minute. As he waited there in the field, his gear feeling heavier by the minute, sweat dripping into his eyes, he heard the chopping sound of an approaching helicopter. To him, this day felt like a day detached from real life, on its own, part of no season or week or month. And all he wanted to do was get his job done well, focus on what he had to do.

The helicopter buzzed the scene, an action normal for emergency helicopters as they scan their landing area, finally stopping to hover a few hundred feet above the school. Its red bottom contrasted with the pure blue of that day's sky, and the chopping noise it made felt out of place, adding, if possible, an even greater sense of urgency to the scene. It would be a long time before Rob, or others in those fields that day, could hear the sound of helicopter blades and not be completely swept away with emotion.

Rob tried to contact that chopper by radio again and again, but with no luck. A sense of impatience rose as Rob attempted to get the helicopter to land. He knew those kids needed to get to the hospital as soon as possible, but the helicopter wasn't coming down. Finally he called 911.

"What frequency are the helicopters on? We're trying to establish communication."

Rob waited while they called the Lancaster airport tower to get the frequency. Meanwhile, he ran over to the Bart Fire Department guys and expressed his frustration about not being able to contact the helicopter. Another helicopter was approaching. These guys needed to land!

At some point, though, the realization sunk in: it was a news helicopter, the first on the scene, and cameras were rolling.

The medical helicopters arrived soon after that. Dust rose around the school as the rotor blades stirred the air. The grass bent under their weight and the trees blew around, four small hurricanes landing, waiting. Once the helicopters were safely on the ground, Rob walked toward the school. The urgent feeling emanating from that small area had not diminished during the minutes he spent preparing the area for the helicopters. The swirling dust and debris caused by the rotating blades gave the scene an even more dramatic feel, as those on the ground ducked their heads and held their hats down while they worked.

Soon Rob and his crew were helping to carry the girls on stretchers to the waiting helicopters and ambulances, based on the assessments done by the paramedics on the scene. Some girls were placed in ambulances and whisked away. It was difficult keeping them straight—who was going where—because they had no identification, most of them were similar in size, and with their solid-colored dresses, straight hair pulled back, and no jewelry it was difficult to differentiate them. Besides, they didn't have time to confirm their identities. These girls needed critical medical attention and they needed it fast.

The school yard was strewn with medical supplies: ripped plastic bags and their paper instructions, discarded on the spot, littered the yard. The departing ambulances and helicopters whipped up the debris in the wake of their sirens and flashing lights. The wounded Amish girls were swept away in the maelstrom, leaving the troopers, EMTs, and firemen to clean up what was left. Once the girls had been evacuated from the school yard, everything suddenly seemed quiet.

Vietta had blood on her hands and clothes, and the school yard swarmed with first responders. The police cleared the scene, directing everyone away from the school. Strangely enough, the sun still shone brilliantly, and a soft breeze crept slowly along the autumn fields.

Some of the Amish neighbors were still gathered along the school yard's white fence, leaning on the white rail, staring blankly at the school or the ground or the sky. Others slowly walked through the field to one of the neighboring farms that served as a meeting place for the community.

Rob watched as one young Amish couple walked slowly across the field, through the shadows of the trees and surrounding barns. Behind them the sun reflected off a bright white barn. The man carried a bag in one hand, his other hand thrust deep into his trousers' pocket. His wife toted a baby in front of her. Their faces were pale and still.

Everyone on the scene seemed stunned.

Rob approached the state police again.

"Is there anything else we can do to help?" he asked.

He was told that he and his men could search the field for evidence. Despite the fact that Charles Roberts was dead, the school was still considered a crime scene, and everything would have to be taken apart piece by piece. So Rob gathered his men, and they formed a long line with the five or six other fire companies that had responded. Fifty or sixty men in all, they stood twenty feet apart and began walking slowly, methodically, through the field toward the farm where the Amish community was gathering. The firemen found a pen and a small piece of fabric, and marked each as evidence. While necessary, the walk for evidence seemed to Rob to be painfully after-the-fact, futile.

Only a few hours prior, those schoolchildren had made their way through those very same fields. Perhaps one of them worried about a troublesome lesson, while another couldn't wait to tell a friend something new. They had converged on that school from all directions, but now a long line of weary men walked those same fields, their eyes searching the ground for any evidence having to do with the shooting that had shattered those children's lives.

As Rob approached the farm, still wearing his fireman's gear and walking in a line, he looked up and saw the crowd of Amish that had gathered there, waiting for information. Some of the families who had girls inside the school were inside the farmhouse, waiting to find out which hospital their girls had been sent to. Some of the boys who had hid behind the outhouses were there, too, looking down with empty eyes toward the school, or up at the helicopters as they rushed toward the horizon. Many in the crowd looked up and watched the men combing the field, wondering if they had any information.

Rob looked down the line of volunteer firemen searching the field. Some of those Amish volunteers, especially the ones from Bart Fire Company, knew these children on a first-name basis. They knew the families. This was their community. What were they thinking as their eyes scanned those fields for pieces of fabric or footprints?

The fire companies completed the search and returned to the schoolhouse, and each step reminded Rob how weary he was, emotionally as much as physically. He and his men waited in a grassy patch close to the school, just to see if there was anything else they could do. Already the Amish from the area were bringing in refreshments and food for the volunteers, more food than they could ever eat. It's something in the blood of the Amish community—when a tragic event occurs, it's as if they know they cannot do anything to change what has happened, but they want to help as much as they can, so they provide the basics that are needed to continue on. For an hour or so, Rob's men sat in the grass. It was a warm day, and with their coats and bunker gear on they had worked up a lather of sweat.

Rob closed his eyes for a moment, trying to escape that scene. But all he could see were blinking lights. It's what he saw at night when he went home after responding to an accident—not the sounds, not the smells of gasoline or burning rubber, but the incessant flash of blue and red and white and yellow lights, constantly barraging his mind, refusing to let him forget what he had just been through.

One group of men gathered around an ambulance. They were strong men, used to seeing injured people. Most of them had seen death before, usually caused by some accident. The group stood there quietly, not speaking. Tears flowed from the eyes of these strong men as they stared into some far-off place. There was anger, too. Frustration that someone would shatter people's lives with such violence and there was nothing they could do about it. Rob noticed many clenched fists.

When Rob and his crew arrived back at the Gap firehouse, a sort of helplessness clung to each of them along with the dust and the sweat. They had decided to pass on the debriefing session being held at the Bart Fire Station. The rush and determination to help had passed. The hectic environment under which they thrive and do their jobs was behind them. Thoughts and reflections on the schoolhouse and what they had seen began creeping into the corners of their minds, and a somber melancholy kept them silent. They sat in the fire hall drinking black coffee, watching the news of the horrible event they had just witnessed with their very eyes, now being broadcast around the world.

But then Rob heard a piece of news he had not heard before. In the craziness of the scene and the speed at which they were forced to operate, there was a detail he'd missed, a detail he now heard for the first time.

All of the victims were girls.

That's when it hit him. Hard. Rob had two daughters of his own. The thought of what had happened suddenly clenched like a hand around his throat. He was done for the day; he dropped his stuff in his locker and went home, where he sat around and stared off into empty spaces. He didn't go to work the next day.

When Vietta got home that night, she turned to her husband and in a shaking voice said, "Nobody is going to make it. None of those girls are going to survive. And I'm never, never, going back. I'm done. I can't do this anymore."

Months later I came across a picture of a small, barefooted Amish girl crouched down on the road beside the grass. She wore a deep blue dress the color of the sky. Wisps of her long hair had come loose from where they had been tied back and were lifted up by the wind and caught by the sun's rays. She stared intently at the ground, perhaps playing in the dirt or watching an insect move slowly along the road.

Above her a long line of fluorescent yellow police tape flipped back and forth in the breeze.

Amish women grieving at the fence

CHAPTER SEVEN

Losing Angie

THE MOMENT I first heard the news of the shootings will stay with me for the rest of my life, much the same way that people remember where they were when they first heard that an airplane had flown into one of the Twin Towers in New York City. It is one of those split seconds in life when I changed—something inside of me grew older, tired, sad.

Sometimes life just does that to you.

I was going to meet my daughter for lunch. The day shone bright blue and was warm for the beginning of October. As I drove up the hill toward the restaurant, I looked to my left, to the north, and out over miles and miles of farmers' fields. Most of them were harvested, a patchwork of green and tan and brown. Beyond the fields, maybe ten miles off, I could see soft, rolling hills covered with trees changing into their fall colors. It was a beautiful day.

Up at the top of that hill the wind is almost always blowing, and when I pulled my pickup truck into the restaurant's parking lot and got out, gusts of wind blew early autumn leaves across the pavement—they weren't deep colors yet, mostly pale yellow with tints of brown or green. Then I saw my daughter LaVale and walked toward her. She smiled, waving at me, her blond hair flying around in the breeze. But there was concern on her face.

"What's wrong?" I asked, putting my arm around her.

"Haven't you heard?" she asked me.

"Heard what?"

"There's been a shooting at an Amish school in Nickel Mines."

The news left me feeling surprised and confused—where had my daughter heard this? Was she sure it was true? Who would ever go into an Amish school with a gun? I found the whole thing very hard to believe. I had grown up in the Amish community. I had been one of those little Amish boys with the straw hats and suspenders, running through the fields barefoot, playing in the large hay barns with my cousins. Having been Amish as a child, having grown up in that kind of tightly knit community, I simply couldn't believe that this kind of evil had made its way into the Amish world. I felt sure the shooter must be from outside the area, perhaps someone from another city or state—certainly no one who knew and lived among the Amish.

Apart from the shock I felt at the news, and the sadness I felt for the families, I also experienced a deep sense of a loss of innocence. For a community like the Amish, so family oriented, to experience something like this, well, I wondered what the effect would be.

Inside the restaurant, the atmosphere was still and eerily quiet. It is normally a busy place, with waitresses flying by and the sounds of a noisy kitchen following them from table to table, but on that morning everyone's attention was fixed on the television behind the small bar. The news was on, the kind with flashing red banners and continuous updates, and the volume was turned up. The shooter had killed himself. At least two children were dead. Numerous more wounded.

So it was true. It had happened to us. During the previous decade we had watched with horror and sadness as shootings like this unfolded in different communities around the country: Columbine, and the sniper in Washington, D.C. But I found it hard to imagine something like this happening in Lancaster County, Pennsylvania. Judging from the comments I overheard, that's how most people felt: even if there was a shooting in one of our community's schools, surely it would not be in an *Amish* schoolhouse. But it had happened, and this time it was Amish blood that was shed . . . our blood.

Two children dead, eight more wounded and in critical condition. Whenever I hear of a child's passing, my thoughts immediately flash back to a moment in my life that will forever shape who I am; the moment that, more than any other, divides my life into two halves: before and after.

• • •

THIRTY-ONE YEARS and twenty-four days before the shooting at the schoolhouse in Nickel Mines, on September 8, 1975, I sat in an office at our church. Two small desks sat against the wall. My wife, Anne, and I worked with the youth group, and I would usually spend Monday mornings at the office, first at a staff meeting and then just catching up on things left over from the weekend services.

Before going to the church that morning we'd had a big breakfast at our house with a group who had been visiting. My wife cooked up a spread of food, and my daughters ran around underfoot—four-year-old LaWonna was eager to go outside and play with her cousins; nineteen-month-old Angie toddled around, speaking her gibberish nonstop and providing the morning's entertainment. She could talk and talk, and most of the time we didn't even know what she was saying, but her voice was pure and innocent and I could listen to her talk all day long.

In spite of living in a small mobile home and making only enough money to live month to month, we were a happy family. My wife's parents lived just up the lane in a large stone house, my brother-in-law and his family lived down the lane from us, and we spent much of our time with family. It was a peaceful life, and when I compare our lives before that day to our lives after that day, it seemed a simple time as well. When I wasn't at the church preparing for youth events I was running my body shop just a few miles away, repairing cars, reversing the effects of accidents and time. It was one of my passions in life, and the business did pretty well for us. I rarely felt unsettled or had any sort of longing for more money. We were content.

That hectic Monday morning went by quickly, and soon I was in the office, enjoying the peace and quiet, getting ready for another week. I don't remember exactly what time it was, but at some point during the morning I heard footsteps coming through the church toward the office. The footsteps were fast, someone urgently crossing the sanctuary. I thought to myself, Something isn't right. There was this feeling in the pit of my stomach that something bad had happened. The door shot open, and I looked up expectantly.

"There's been an accident. Angie is hurt, she's at the clinic."

There were no other details. I pictured Angie, with her blond curls and blue eyes, talking incessantly. My insides sunk and the blood left my face. In an instant I felt numb. In that moment nothing else mattered: not the work I had been doing, not the cars at the body shop, not the long to-do list. I ran out the door and headed for the local clinic, only a few miles away.

I can still picture the front of that clinic on the day of Angie's accident: large glass doors under a peaked roof, with bushes on either side. Strange—it was also a Monday morning, but in September, not October, and I was thirty years younger, in my late twenties—practically still a kid. There at the glass doors stood Anne. She was barefoot. She looked out of place and almost comical in her bathrobe, but nothing about her expression looked silly in the least—there was a look on her face that I had never seen before, and it scared me. It was as if someone had taken the soul out of her, leaving only flesh and bones. No spirit or life.

"She's gone," she said in a hoarse whisper, her face heavy with despair. "Angie's dead."

How can you process that kind of information? How can you take a fact so horrible in its essence and digest it, let it sink into your mind, without getting physically sick? I drew Anne toward me and held her because it seemed the right thing to do, but inside I felt myself fall into a daze. I lived in that fog for months, maybe years. We are so unprepared for moments like that, and when they happen it is difficult to predict how we will react emotionally.

Sobs threatened to split Anne's small body in two. I don't remember if I cried at that moment. There was just this immense emptiness—nothing else in life held any meaning at that point. Anne held my hand and led me into the clinic. I followed her on complete autopilot, a robot, through the glass doors and into the dimly lit building.

We walked inside and made our way down the corridor to the room where Angie's body lay. It was still morning, maybe eight or nine o'clock, I'm not sure. How quickly life can change. Only a few hours before, I had been rejoicing in a beautiful day, working hard at the church I loved, feeling so content with life. Then, in the blink of an eye, I was walking into the room that held my daughter's dead body.

In the middle of the room was a small examination table, and on it lay Angie's body, covered by a white sheet. I could see the outline of her tiny face, pulled tight and flat by the sheet. One of her little nineteen-month-old hands wasn't covered—do you know how small a toddler's hand looks at that age? Only two or three inches long, her small hand still appeared perfect, but her pale skin looked completely colorless, matching the whiteness of the sheet.

I reached down and held on to her hand, felt her tiny fingers. They were still warm. The nurse came in and allowed us to pull the sheet down and uncover her face—Angie still looked perfect. Her golden hair swirled around her head in beautiful curls. I could not comprehend that she was gone.

Anne held on tight, her arms wrapped around me. Suddenly she looked up at me and asked why we couldn't pray for her. If we prayed, and truly believed, couldn't God bring her back to us? Anne's face was desperate. I was scared at what I saw in her eyes: a sadness I had never encountered before.

I looked down at Angie. She looked so peaceful, lying there. I thought about the verse in 2 Corinthians that talks about how being absent from the body means to be present with the Lord, and for a moment I pictured her walking along grassy slopes in heaven, approaching some far-off golden city.

"She is where we want to be someday," I said quietly to Anne, barely able to speak through the tears and the ache in my throat. "Do you really want to bring her back to this? This pain and sorrow?"

We stood there for a long time in that small examination room at the clinic. On our way back home I learned that my sister-in-law Fi had backed one of the small tractors out of the barn and hadn't seen Angie running up the lane to her grand-mother's house. Angie's tiny body was no match for the slowly backing tractor. I still couldn't believe it. Angie was gone.

EATING LUNCH with LaVale, I watched the news coming at us from the television behind the bar. I drank some coffee and stared into the cup. If anyone in the restaurant spoke, it was in hushed tones. Some of the waitresses looked like they might start crying. I sighed.

"I'd better get going," I said. "I've got a meeting coming up."

I left some money on the table, and then LaVale and I walked outside. I hugged her, perhaps a little closer than usual, thinking of those parents who were just coming to grips with the news that their child might be gone, thinking of Angie. There is nothing I have experienced more heart wrenching or mentally disorienting than having my child die before I did. It is an event completely contrary to the natural cycle of things. Yet it happens, and we are left holding the numerous, jagged-edged pieces of our lives, won-dering if they will ever fit back together.

I got into my truck, drove across the countryside on back roads that wound and rose and dipped across the fields and hills toward my office. It was a beautiful fall day, and the air gushing in my window smelled of autumn and harvest. I turned on the radio to listen to the news, but the voices just drifted past me. I was so far from that place and time. It never ceases to amaze me how certain things can trigger emotions from over thirty years ago.

Those emotions feel so fresh, as if the event had just happened and I was experiencing it for the first time.

JUST AS my meeting started, I got a call. It was my brother-in-law Mike.

"Hi, Jonas, where are you?" he asked me.

"I'm here at a meeting. Have you heard about the shooting in Nickel Mines? What's going on over there?"

"I'm here at the King family farm, right across the field from the school," he said, his voice trembling slightly.

"Okay," I said. "I know where that is."

"Jonas," he said, pausing for a moment before continuing. "I think you should be here."

It took me only a moment to make the decision. I offered my apologies to the man I was meeting with, explained the situation. He understood. Before I knew it I was back in my truck, driving the winding roads through the countryside once again, this time going toward the Amish school in Nickel Mines. I wondered what I would find when I arrived.

The whole way there I listened to the news, but once again I found it difficult to concentrate on what was being discussed. Ten children shot. The shooter dead. Such an immense waste of life. My mind wandered to the parents. I remembered what it felt like to live through those first horrifying moments. In fact, I was living through them again: the moment I found out Angie was in an accident, the moment Anne told me she was gone, and the moment I saw Angie for myself, lying peacefully on an examination table in a small country clinic.

I thought of the process the parents of these girls would encounter, the many years of difficult moments ahead of them. I thought of the numbness that comes in those first few hours and days and weeks. The sharp points of despair and anguish that sometimes threaten to take you over the edge. There are times, many long years later, when the event lies in the past but still lends a weight to your heart that never goes away. The accident, the event, is one thing, but the long road they had ahead of them filled me with a sense of such deep sorrow and heaviness that I found my eyes filling with tears as I drove.

Twenty minutes later I saw a roadblock: some orange barriers placed in the roadway, flanked by some local police and first responders. They were keeping people from driving too close to the schoolhouse or filling up the roads and blocking emergency workers. I wondered if they would let me through. I pulled up slowly, then stopped and leaned my head out the window.

One of the men at the roadblock recognized me and knew I had founded the counseling center.

"Oh, hi, Jonas. Thanks for coming," he said, as he pulled the barrier aside and let me through.

Another half mile down the road there was another roadblock.

"Hi, I'm Jonas Beiler from the Family Resource and Counseling Center," I began.

"Oh, yeah," the man said. "I've heard of your counseling center. You need to be in there."

He, too, pulled the barrier aside and let me through.

As I approached the school, coming up on Mine Road, I saw a strange sight: five news helicopters circled in the beautiful blue sky over the open fields. The chopping sound of their blades seemed distant and otherworldly.

I came up Mine Road but couldn't turn onto White Oak to get close to the school, so I pulled down a long stone lane bordered by cornfields that led to the King farm, where Mike said he was waiting. The field rose on a small hill between the farm and the school, but the corn was cut and I could just barely see the schoolhouse and the tree beside it. What I could see was all movement—police officers walking around the property, firemen cleaning up around the scene, EMTs putting equipment back into their ambulances.

Not even three hours had passed, but already there were over one hundred Amish folks from the community standing around at the farm trying to get updates. The women had their arms around one another, and the men stood in close circles, their hands in their pockets, talking quietly. More were on the way—I could see them walking across the fields or arriving in horse and buggies.

The families of the girls were gathered in the farmhouse, mostly trying to find out which hospitals their girls had been taken to. Despite the fact that I grew up Amish, and still often dealt with members of their community, I was still amazed at how quickly they had come together to support one another. This is the Amish response to tragedy—quick, thorough, and overwhelming in the most positive sense. I suddenly felt an enormous warmth for them, as well as for my heritage, rise inside of me. If there is one thing you can guarantee about the Amish, it's that they will not allow anyone in their community to suffer a tragedy on their own.

Soon I saw two older couples outside the farm. They were the grandparents of some of the girls who had been shot. I heard them telling some of those waiting outside that the parents were having trouble finding out which girls had been taken to which hospitals. When the medical helicopters had arrived and whisked the girls away, it had been nearly impossible to tell the girls apart due to numerous factors: the frantic nature of the scene, the number of victims, their similar age and dress, and the fact that the nature of their injuries meant it was difficult to describe their facial features. Eventually the hospitals would take digital photos of the girls, blacking out their injuries, and e-mail them to someone on the scene who passed the pictures on to the parents. Even then, some of the parents would go to the wrong hospitals.

I remember when I was a child and our neighbor's barn burned down—the firemen fought the blaze all through the night and into the morning. Before they even finished hosing down the glowing embers, the local community was there, lumber for the new barn was delivered, and one of our Amish neighbors, serving as contractor, had the plans for a new barn out on the kitchen table. The men arrived later that day to begin building. The women arrived with more food than everyone could possibly eat, setting it onto rows of tables where we could all help ourselves. The staccato beat of a community's worth of hammers sounded out all day, and the barn was rebuilt in no time. Many hands make light work, we always used to say.

As I got out of my vehicle and headed into the crowd, I felt two emotions very deeply: I was imagining, once again, what a long road these families had in front of them. But I was also surrounded by this sense of being in such a rich culture. Some of the things they were already doing are woven deep in them from birth: they had assembled like this so quickly, the men standing in one main area, the women grieving together in another; the parents and families of the girls, those most deeply affected, were protected in the confines of the house, surrounded by those closest to them, waiting to hear if their children had survived.

Still looking for Mike, I walked up to a group of Amish men. They stood in their work clothes, black trousers with suspenders over plain-colored shirts. Their beards were grown free but the hair above their top lips was shaved. They wore straw hats. Many just kept shaking their heads at the horror of what had happened only a few hours ago.

"Has anyone done anything to help you manage the media?" I asked no one in particular. I looked up again at the helicopters circling in the sky, pointing their cameras down at the Amish who had gathered, and it just didn't seem right. It wasn't how things should be. They are such a private people, and I felt they deserved the honor and dignity of some kind of space.

I'm not sure that the group of men understood my point. They certainly had no way of comprehending the media onslaught that was already on the way. I don't think any of us did.

After a short conversation, we all stood around together, in shock. By this time they knew the shooter had been Charles Roberts. Most of them knew who he was—he served as milkman for many of the families in that area, including some of the families of the girls he had shot. There was profound confusion regarding why someone from inside their community would do something so unimaginable.

Just then I saw a media van driving up a dirt lane through the field, approaching the farmhouse. Suddenly it stopped, turned around, and drove back out. Then a lone news photographer began approaching, stopping every now and then to take some pictures before slowly advancing another twenty paces and taking some more. I kept watching him. I know the media need to do their jobs, but it seemed so intrusive that I was about to ask him to take a hike, but a state trooper did the job for me.

I didn't even realize the police were there, but learned that one trooper was stationed in the house and two outside to keep the media at bay. Even with the volunteers blocking the incoming roads, the journalists somehow found their way through the maze of farm lanes and fields to the center of the tragedy.

The whole atmosphere felt so sad and empty. Questions hung in the air, as awkward as those helicopters; questions that many of the Amish may have felt uncomfortable with. Why? Why would this happen to such innocent little girls? What could have possibly caused someone to commit such a heinous act?

Through the rumor mill of the crowd I heard that some of the grandparents wanted to go to the fire hall, a mile or so up the road, to help figure out where each of the children had been taken, and I offered to give them a ride. Just before we left the King farm, the grandparents were giving details to the police to try to identify the girls: eye color, dress color if they could remember, hair color, birthmarks, height and weight, and other details. Once again I was hit by the innocence of these children as their approximate weights were given, some only fifty or sixty pounds.

I drove slowly down Mine Road toward the fire hall with two passengers in my car—by that time the road was reduced to one lane due to all the television trucks and vans—and passed White Oak Road, the street that led to the school. It was blocked by policemen. Through a few trees and over the corn I could see the schoolhouse with the truck driven by Charles Roberts still backed up to the front door where he had left it.

We continued straight on Mine Road, then made a short right toward the Bart fire hall. The grandparents thanked me for the ride and walked inside. I parked down the street, then followed after them, entering the already bustling fire hall.

First responders were straggling back into the hall looking exhausted and stunned by the morning's events. Volunteers, some Amish, were serving food to them. The first responders' eyes looked empty and sad, and I could only imagine what they had seen inside that schoolhouse.

Buggy passing a media horde

CHAPTER EIGHT

Think No Evil

I POURED MYSELF a cup of coffee at the Bart fire hall and took in the scene. The debriefings had started—groups of first responders were going into some of the side rooms and offices in the fire hall to talk about what they had been through. As counselors, we have seen a vast difference in the long-term emotional health of first responders who receive an initial debriefing and those who do not. I was not involved in any of the meetings that day, so I wandered around the fire hall, listening to any bystanders who just needed to talk.

I ran into Brad Aldrich while I was there. Brad is the executive director of the Family Resource and Counseling Center, which we had founded fifteen years prior. Brad started at the center as a counselor and grew into the position of director, where his roles included public relations and fund-raising. On that day, he had been at his office, looking over some paperwork and preparing for his individual meetings with other counselors. When he first heard the news, his mind couldn't register the information. A shooting at an Amish school. Only miles away. Then came the blur of activity as the counseling center's phones began to ring. Everyone in the center had questions with no answers: Which school? How far away? Was the shooter on the loose? Many of our counselors grabbed their coats off the backs of their chairs with the intention of driving to the scene to help, but Brad stepped in. They knew nothing about the shooter's status or even if the scene was safe. He decided that two counselors would join him on a trip to find the school and the rest would remain at the center, wait for a report back, and handle the influx of calls into the center.

When Brad first saw the schoolhouse it was a blaze of activity: what seemed like hundreds of state patrol cars, ambulances, fire trucks, and all of their associated personnel surrounded the small building. Brad noticed that the King farm, about a half mile off in the distance, seemed to be the center of activity for the Amish, so he drove in that direction. He parked his car along Mine Road and walked up the lane toward the farm, wondering what he would encounter. At this point Brad knew very little about what had actually happened. He only knew there was a gunman. He had no idea if anyone had been shot or, if she had, how badly injured anyone might be.

When he spoke with the Amish families mingling outside of the farmhouse, none of them yet knew the full events. There were whispers of a hostage situation. A man with a gun. But everything was still rumor, and not much news was coming from the school, or from the families still waiting in the farmhouse.

As more ambulances and fire trucks arrived, and the helicopters began to circle, the mood at the farm grew increasingly somber. Amish men stood closer together and their voices took on hushed tones. The name of Charles Roberts began to circulate. Perhaps one of the freed boys recognized him from his milk route. Everyone tried to figure out why someone from their own community would do this. Did someone know of any arguments or disagreements he may have had? Was he a violent man by nature? Had he ever done anything strange before? Again, too many unanswered questions left the gathering crowd feeling helpless and despondent.

Even Brad became more and more reflective as he wandered around the yard. Clouds of dust swept across the harvested cornfields as fire trucks and ambulances screamed down Mine Road and helicopters hovered toward a landing area between the farm and the school. Autumn leaves blew across the dirt lane and crunched under Brad's feet. As he looked down the farm lane he saw the boys from the schoolhouse, the boys whom Charles had released.

Their first stop after being released from the school was just behind the outhouses beside the school. They didn't want to leave their fellow classmates, but couldn't go back inside, so they waited there. The Amish are a deeply religious community, so even those young boys began praying for their sisters and friends. Soon the police arrived and quickly ushered them across the field to safety. Then, in the maelstrom of the scene and the rising concern for the remaining students, they were left, forgotten for a moment.

This is when Brad found them.

The Amish boys sat in one long, straight line along the farm lane. Brad wondered if they had been there when he arrived—if so, he had walked right by them without even noticing. It would have been easy to miss them. They sat quietly, perfectly still, staring at the blue sky, the fields, the dirt lane, not saying a word.

There were about twelve boys and one girl, ages five to twelve; the boys all had their elbows on their knees, some with their faces in their hands. Their eyes had that wide-open look, a mixture of fear, confusion, and sadness. There was nothing for them to do, so they sat there quietly, waiting, frozen in place.

Brad saw a group of what appeared to be fathers standing around up the lane a bit, so he approached them.

"Hi," he said quietly. "I'm Brad Aldrich from the counseling center. Would it be okay with you if I went over and had a word with the boys for a couple of minutes?"

The men nodded their heads, some of them looking relieved and appreciative, so Brad made his way over to the boys and sat down in the grass with them. He asked them how they were doing. He got a few names. He asked them about school and other things that Amish boys their age would talk about. Brad had no idea what had just happened or what these boys had seen, so he was just opening lines of communication.

As Brad continued to chat with the kids, something suddenly

clicked in his mind: Where were all the girls? There was one little girl sitting with the boys, but he was pretty sure that a school that size would have more than just one girl.

Some of the older boys began hinting more and more at the events in the school: the man had a gun, they were scared, and the younger kids were confused, even more so than the older ones. Brad began to sense that they had seen something pretty horrible and, in the simplest of terms, tried to help them understand what they might be feeling or thinking.

"You might have a knot in the pit of your stomach, or you might feel sick. You might feel very tired, or you might not feel different at all, for a little while. It's okay."

Mentally he began evaluating each of the children for signs of shock. As the seriousness of the incident became clear, he wondered how they were even functioning.

The sun was getting hot, so Brad suggested that they go get some water and something to eat. He knew they must be holding a lot inside and wanted to reassure them somehow.

"You do what you want to do, okay?" Brad told the children. "If you want to go play, go play. If you want to take a nap, take a nap. If you want to sit quietly, that's okay."

As the children vanished into the crowd of Amish, Brad was approached by two state policemen.

"Where did you just send those kids? We've been waiting for an hour to talk to them about what happened."

"Don't worry," Brad said quietly. "They're just getting some lunch. They're only kids. They might need a little space right now. They'll be right back."

Once the police were on the scene it didn't look like Brad would be able to speak to the boys any longer, so he decided to drive over to Bart fire hall, the staging point for the fire and ambulance crews. He knew there would be more people in need of help over there.

But as he headed for the fire hall, he couldn't get that picture out of his mind: the line of boys sitting quietly along the dirt lane. It was yet another example of the community's innocence coming under fire, the fact that those boys had to go through the terror of that morning. Brad wondered how the Amish would respond to such a direct assault on their children.

When Brad walked into the Bart Township fire hall the first thing he noticed was how quiet it was, especially considering there were at least one hundred people milling around. A few standing on the room's fringes watched the news broadcasts on small televisions, but it seemed that more of those present were avoiding the news. The images being broadcast around the world were ones they had just seen firsthand, and they didn't need to have them reinforced or projected into their minds from yet another angle.

The film crews were not allowed in the fire hall, but during his short drive over Brad had traveled through a line of countless media vans and reporters. This is really a huge story, he thought to himself after seeing the multitude of news cameras pointing their lenses at the school. Brad still knew very little about what had happened in the schoolhouse. He knew there had been a gun. He knew shots had been fired. That was it.

Then the debriefings started. Those who had been involved on the scene were invited to the Bart fire hall to talk with counselors about what they had seen and how it had affected them. The counselors then told them what they might expect to encounter over the coming days and weeks, both emotionally and physically, and what they could do to cope with it. When Brad met with the Christiana ambulance crew, Vietta and Samantha, he suddenly encountered the horror that had unfolded in the school. They spoke bluntly about gruesome injuries—shots to the head, massive blood loss, gaping wounds. Brad began getting a sense of what these people had seen, and felt a heaviness for them.

Later in the day Brad found himself sitting with a paramedic who had been forced to make some difficult calls regarding treatment. When he walked in for his debriefing he still had dark red flecks all over his stethoscope, and his shirt had larger red stains. He looked beaten up, both physically exhausted and emotionally spent.

"That's the first time I've ever had to make these kinds of decisions about who gets treated and who doesn't," the man sighed to Brad. "I actually had to say, 'Don't bother treating that one, she's not going to make it, we have to focus on saving the others.' Don't get me wrong, I've seen death before, but at most it's usually four people in a car accident and there's enough of us to help out all four of them. Even if one of those four isn't going to make it we still do what we can. But there just weren't enough of us. We couldn't work on all of the girls. I had to make some pretty tough decisions."

The man's head dropped and he stared at the floor, his shoulders sagging.

By the time Brad left the fire hall, the street was completely lined with news vans and satellite dishes. There wasn't room for one more vehicle in their midst, and still more stations were arriving, literally from around the world, parking at the end of the line, dragging their cables into neighbors' houses, and plugging in. Correspondents stood shoulder to shoulder, conveying the horrible news in somber tones and serious looks. Cameramen swiveled quickly to catch a shot of a passing buggy. They zoomed in for a shot of Amish people walking through the fields or of the square plot of land holding the schoolhouse, by then cordoned off with yellow police tape.

Brad and his staff drove slowly through this traffic back out to the King farm and counseled the women who had been in the school when Charles entered. There were still over fifty Amish people at the farm. Brad spoke with some of the men mingling around outside—cousins, uncles, and other extended family. They spoke about the events of the day, and about the line of media trucks now completely lining the road from the farm to the corner by the auction house.

You would think that such an invasion of television cameras and trucks with satellite dishes perched on their roofs would be intimidating to the Amish, but at that point the Amish response to the media was mostly favorable—they were glad the word was getting out so that people could pray for them. One of the Amish families had missionary friends in Africa who called them that afternoon because they saw the news coverage. They were amazed at how the media were helping them to connect with friends from around the world.

Brad also asked some of the older Amish men for guidance on how he should represent their community to the media. How should he answer their questions about the shooting, about the Amish faith, and about their community? The Amish response was mostly unified on this—as long as it was getting out the word of God, and bearing positive witness to their belief in Christ, then they were all for it.

One of the Amish men came over to Brad toward the end of the evening. His eyes were tired from a long day of crying and looking for hope. Without even speaking, the expression on his face seemed to say, "Now I have seen everything." There was also an underlying current of unease about him. Soon Brad discovered the source.

"I don't even want to ask the question 'why?' " he said to Brad. "But I still wouldn't mind knowing."

The look in the man's eyes reminded Brad of earlier in the day, when he had debriefed bystanders, some of the Amish neighbors who had been on the scene, and a few firefighters, all together in one group. The atmosphere in the room had been subdued, and when someone spoke, everyone had listened intently. Some of the voices sounded soft, like a dulled edge, while others were constantly catching with emotion.

One of the Amish men in the meeting raised a question.

"Do we know why he went to this school instead of one of the four other schools close by?"

"Not yet," Brad had said.

Brad could sense everyone mulling that question in their own minds, the randomness of the act, the possibility that it could have been their own child's school.

A few of the men commented about Charles Roberts—they were not hateful comments, but mostly probing questions wondering how someone could do what he had done. There was some anger, some frustration, and a lot of sadness. Toward the end of the discussion one person in the group, who was not Amish, said to the Amish men, "It should be a relief to you that he's dead, he's gone, and he's not going to do this again."

Silence filled the room.

In any typical post-shooting environment, this statement would most likely be accepted and even amplified: "Yeah, good riddance!" Most of us, quite naturally, would be relieved that someone who had committed such a horrible atrocity was no longer around. In a close-knit community such as Nickel Mines you would think that people would be thankful they wouldn't have to relive the incident with a trial and that they would never have to see this man alive again.

That's not how the Amish think.

Brad could see it on one Amish man's face, how inappropriate he found that comment. The man didn't say anything, but his jaw clenched in disagreement, and his eyes looked pained.

This Amish man's first response was not to look for relief or to be thankful for some apparent working of cosmic justice where the evil man gets what he deserves—his first response was forgiveness and a longing for reconciliation. For the first time that day, Brad felt the overwhelming nature of Amish forgiveness.

Brad knew the Amish were a peaceful people, but when he saw the hurt in that man's eyes, genuine hurt for Charlie's death, he understood just how far their forgiveness would go. In the days to come we would learn more about specific acts of forgiveness demonstrated by the Amish toward the family of Charles Roberts, but already the media were seeing something different in this story compared to other tragic shootings: an absence of malice toward the shooter or his family. The press began to arrive even as the girls were being carried from the schoolhouse and stayed to cover the aftermath of this event. They understood the grief that they saw in the Amish, but they were not prepared for the overwhelming and universal display of concern for the Roberts family. Word had leaked out that an Amish neighbor went to the home of the shooter that very night to let his wife know that they bore no hard feelings toward her or even her husband. There was even talk going around that the families of the ten little girls wanted to meet with the Roberts family to express their forgiveness.

I LEFT the fire hall that evening at about the same time Brad was finishing up his debriefings at the farm. I believe I was experiencing what everyone in the community was experiencing: shock, disbelief that something like this had happened so close to home, and sadness for the girls and their families. The night was closing in and the air was getting cool. I was driving home, thinking about the day and about my daughter Angie when my cell phone rang.

I looked down at it, feeling tired and not wanting to talk unless it was Anne or one of my girls. To my surprise, the caller ID on my phone said "NBC." I realized that a good friend of mine with connections in the media had given my number to some different folks who were looking for someone to interview. I guess because I was a counselor, grew up Amish, and still had connections to the Amish community, I was an ideal person to talk to. I answered my phone.

"Ann Curry would like to come to your house and get a statement about forgiveness," said the person on the phone.

It was at that point that I started to realize how interested the rest of the world was in the unique response of the Amish to the tragedy that had found its way into their midst. I don't know if I had consciously thought about it before that call—a forgiving response is programmed into the Amish, so it didn't seem remarkable to me in the least. I knew that folks from outside our area would be intrigued when they saw how the Amish dressed, or how they traveled in their buggies, or how their lifestyle of simplicity didn't include modern conveniences. But I hadn't thought about how their quick forgiveness would command such an immediate and extensive audience.

"Sure," I said, "come on over."

As soon as I got off the phone with them I called my wife.

"Just thought I should let you know that Ann Curry from NBC is coming over tonight," I said.

"No, she's not," my wife said in disbelief.

"Yeah, she is. In fact she'll be over in about thirty minutes."

What struck me the most about our brief interview was how quickly Ann Curry zeroed in on forgiveness. Once again I could see that theme rising to prominence, like a bright red thread winding its way through a white carpet. To this day, the irony almost makes me smile: I think of how most Amish had probably never heard of Ann Curry, yet their Christian message of radical, no-strings-attached forgiveness brought her from New York City to Nickel Mines so that she could tell the rest of the world about it.

The media clearly realized that something different was going on. There was an element to this tragedy that didn't follow the normal script. The first thing that garnered the public's attention was the Amish's refusal to hold a grudge of any kind against Charles's family:

> In just about any other community, a deadly school shooting would have brought demands from civic leaders for tighter gun laws and better security, and the victims' loved ones would have lashed out at the gunman's family or threatened to sue.
>
> But that's not the Amish way.
>
> As they struggle with the slayings of five of their children in a one-room schoolhouse, the Amish in this Lancaster County village are turning the other cheek, urging forgiveness of the killer, and quietly accepting what comes their way as God's will.
>
> "They know their children are going to heaven. They know their children are innocent . . . and they know that they will join them in death," said Gertrude Huntington, a Michigan researcher and expert on children in Amish society.

"The hurt is very great," Huntington said. "But they don't balance the hurt with the hate."

In the aftermath of Monday's violence, the Amish are looking inward, relying on themselves and their faith, just as they have for centuries . . .

The Amish have also been reaching out to the family of the gunman, Charles Carl Roberts IV, 32, who committed suicide during the attack.

"The Amish neighbor came that very night, around 9 o'clock in the evening, and offered forgiveness to the family," Dwight Lefever, a Roberts family spokesman said.

"I hope [the Roberts family] stays around here and they'll have a lot of friends and a lot of support," Daniel Esh, a fifty-seven-year-old Amish artist and woodworker whose three grandnephews were inside the school during the attack, said.[1]

You see, for the Amish, it's not enough just to forgive. With their forgiveness they offer reconciliation—an invitation to be in a relationship, to be friends. As a counselor, I always remind people that reconciliation is not a requirement for forgiveness. Some people feel that if they are unable to reconcile with the person who has wronged them, they are not practicing forgiveness. Nothing could be further from the truth, as sometimes it's just too difficult to reconcile with those who have hurt you. But reconciliation can often aid in restoring the emotional health of both the perpetrator and the victim and should at least be attempted whenever it is practical. The Amish almost always offer reconciliation with their forgiveness, as they demonstrated with the Roberts family. But forgiveness was offered not only to Charlie's family. It was also offered to Charlie, as much as it could be, after his death. This attitude may have been the main source of fascination for the media and those unfamiliar with the Amish, and perhaps the best illustration came from a grandfather in the community:

> A grieving grandfather told young relatives not to hate the gunman who killed five girls in an Amish schoolhouse massacre, a pastor said on Wednesday.
>
> "As we were standing next to the body of this thirteen-year-old girl, the grandfather was tutoring the young boys, he was making a point, just saying to the family, 'We must not think evil of this man,' " the Rev. Robert Schenck told CNN.
>
> "It was one of the most touching things I have seen in twenty-five years of Christian ministry."[2]

We must not think evil of this man. Not only were the Amish determined not to act out in any way against Charles Roberts or his family, they were determined to make sure their children did not get caught up in the cycle of hate and retribution.

A new generation of Amish was being shown how to live when life seemed so unfair. Hearing of that grandfather modeling forgiveness to those young boys, I thought back to a lesson I had learned from my own father.

Two Amish men walking down the road

CHAPTER NINE

Godly Examples

MY WIFE AND I were spending a few days at a cabin with some other couples in the summer of 1967. My brother Sonny and his new bride, Edna, were there, and another couple, Bob and my sister Anna. We were about a four-hour drive from our homes and having a lot of fun, getting away from normal life and spending time outdoors. There was a small town close by, but the cabin was fairly isolated and rustic— we had running water but no telephone.

Sonny and I were two years apart, and even though we had our own sets of friends we were extremely close. We owned a business together and had both decided to leave the Amish at about the same time. After Anne and I started dating, we enjoyed many great times with Sonny and Edna, hanging out as couples quite a bit. On this trip, Sonny and Edna were with us for most of the week, but they left for home a day early. We didn't think too much of their early departure from the cabin—I think Sonny needed to go home to do some work.

It was a Monday morning. Bob went down to the store in town to pick up a few things for the cabin, maybe some food, and also to grab a daily paper like he did every morning. Everyone from home knew they could reach us through the telephone at the store. Someone, I think it might have been Bob's mom, left a message at the store that there was an emergency and we were to call home. Bob must have called his mom while he was there because that's how he got the news.

He rushed back to the cabin and told us.

Sonny was dead.

I can't even remember exactly how he said it, what his words were, or what I said back to him. Most of that day—August 7, 1967—and the rest of that week are blurred by too many years. I do remember how I felt: confused and disoriented, much like I would feel nearly ten years later, when Anne, standing in her nightgown outside the clinic, would tell me that Angie was gone.

I don't remember saying a word during the four hours it took to drive home. The silence was only broken by my occasional outbursts of grief. Anne was sad, too, but I think she was more worried about how I would deal with the loss of my brother. Sonny and I weren't just brothers; we were each other's best friend. We hung out together, ran our body shop together, got into a lot of trouble together. I remember wondering how long it had taken the news to get to us, and how strange it was that even after he was dead we had all been sleeping and having a normal day, at least until we got the news.

Once I got home I found out that Sonny had been on his motorcycle when the accident occurred, although to this day we don't know exactly how it happened. A large truck came around a bend on Mast Road, a quarter-mile from our house. The road was pretty narrow. Sonny came from the other direction, and the truck driver wasn't sure how it happened, but they collided. Sonny died instantly.

Something else happened instantly. Strange as it may seem, from the very day of Sonny's death, my grieving parents began contacting that truck driver, checking to see how he was doing. They even invited him to Sonny's funeral. This is always the first response of the Amish community when a tragedy occurs—they always reach out, concerned for how another person is coping, doing everything they can to ease the person's grief, even if that person's actions caused the tragedy.

Like my parents, I never felt angry at the truck driver for what had happened—I guess that's the Amish upbringing coming through. There's something about the way they live that refuses to place blame on people for accidents that happen, even tragic accidents. I have heard many Amish people say, after losing a loved one in an accident, not that the person was in the wrong place at the wrong time, but that they were in the *right* place at the *right* time. God is in control, they say, and it must have been that person's time to go to heaven.

If I felt angry at anyone, it would have been at Sonny. He was one of those stereotypically reckless guys in their early twenties. Some of the things he got us into scared me to no end. He had wrecked multiple vehicles, gotten into all kinds of trouble, and had been the biggest practical joker I knew. I had a hard time believing that the accident hadn't been caused by one of his crazy stunts. I don't know that for a fact, and it may not have been the case at all, yet I couldn't help but wonder.

Yet it was this wild and crazy approach to life that had made him seem so alive. When he died, I became a different person, in a way, because his recklessness had brought out a side of my personality that would not have come out on its own. I was deeply saddened by his death, and it took me many years to come to grips with his absence. When Anne and I got married, about one year later, I remember leaving the sanctuary of the church with her and walking outside—we were laughing and crying at the same time, so happy to be married, and so sad that Sonny couldn't be there with us.

During the days and weeks following Sonny's accident, my parents continued to pursue a friendship with the man who had driven the truck that killed my brother. One evening they took him out to eat, and soon it became an annual tradition for them: my parents would have the man to their house for dinner or take him out to eat, and after they finished their meal they would go by the greenhouse and nursery the man owned. He would allow my parents to pick out any plants or trees they wanted. For years they met this way.

I never got to know the man, but my parents always mentioned it to me when they came home from an evening with him—and they would show me their newest plant or tree. It seemed like the right way to live and the right way to remember Sonny: not with lonely evenings filled with anger and bitterness, but in community, with new friendship, sharing a meal together and relentlessly pursuing reconciliation.

This is also a perfect example of how the Amish culture influences younger generations. I was in my early twenties when Sonny died—if my parents had shown extreme anger or a desire for revenge on the truck driver, it may have steered me down that road as well. But when I saw the way they instantly forgave him it left me with no other inclination but to follow their lead. It's something I'm extremely grateful for, my Amish roots, and I hope that somehow I can pass on this heritage to my children and grandchildren.

FORGIVENESS. THE Encarta Dictionary defines it as the act of pardoning someone for a mistake or wrongdoing.[1] While there are many ways that we can be wronged, there are only two very distinct choices we can make after we are wronged: to forgive or to accuse. In the instance of my own daughter's death, forgiving my sister-in-law felt less like a choice and more like a natural response, probably because of the nature of my relationship with my sister-in-law, my deep faith, and my having grown up in a culture of forgiveness. I do not recall my parents ever *telling* me much about forgiveness, but they showed me how it worked by their actions. That's the Amish way.

Just as important as forgiveness is in helping the Amish move on with their own lives, their decision to forgive can also help those who cause a tragedy recover from their own guilt and pain. This is clearly what happened to a man named Amos, whom I met during the construction of our latest project, the Family Center of Gap. He knew that Anne and I had lost a child, and shared this story with me.

It was May 17, 2004, and Amos was given the day off work by his employer, a local electrical company. One of the perks of working for that particular company was that it gave all of its employees their birthday off, so Amos enjoyed a morning at home and then was off running some errands, just odds and ends, the type of thing anyone does on his day off. We always remember our own birthdays, but something would happen that day that would make Amos wish he could forget it.

Amos was a quiet man with a thin build and dark hair lined with streaks of gray. He had a gentle face, and when he walked from here to there he moved so easily that you could almost miss him, even if he walked right across your path. He rarely talked about that day, but when he did his words flowed together in a slow rhythm, and his voice rolled with a subdued sort of awe, as if he couldn't believe he had lived through it, as if his talking about it in that way would somehow make it all just a dream.

But it wasn't a dream. He had stopped by an Amish neighbor's place to drop off some things. As he pulled into the lane, he never saw the little girl. She was hearing impaired, probably never heard the truck, and darted out in front of it. He didn't see her at all, only felt something, the smallest of somethings, barely anything. He had no idea that the small bump was a child. Her name was Ruthie.

Amos told me how he had stood in the driveway moments after the event, wondering how it had come to pass. He never stopped wondering why he went on that particular day. It could have been any day. It could have been that weekend, or the weekend before. He could have stopped by any evening after work. But for whatever reason, he chose that day, when Ruthie was playing near the driveway.

Right after the accident happened, the father of that little Amish girl sat there in the driveway beside Amos, holding her in his arms. The sun shone brightly, and Amos found himself on his knees beside the man, shaking. They waited for the ambulance to come, and everything was eerily quiet, especially the small girl in the man's arms. The father, holding his little girl, who looked like she may have already died, stared straight into Amos's eyes and spoke words that Amos could barely comprehend.

"You know," he said firmly, "it's not your fault. There wasn't anything you could have done. You didn't do anything wrong. You are not a bad guy."

At the time, Amos couldn't believe what he was hearing. How could any father forgive someone who had just run over his little daughter? It was as if the man was more concerned about Amos than his daughter. Soon the ambulance screamed its way up the drive and came to a quick halt. The paramedics leaped out and swept the little girl away to the hospital, but it was too late. She had died.

After the accident, Amos spoke with the police officer on the scene and then went home. His body felt numb and his brain kept running in a loop, replaying the events over and over again. Pulling into the driveway. Watching, as he always did, for kids who might be playing in the yard. That smallest of bumps. He didn't want to talk to anyone, and since the house was empty he went to bed, lying in the darkness, trying to sleep. But whenever he closed his eyes, all he saw were scenes from the accident: the little girl lying under his truck, the Amish man's face full of despair and sadness, the ambulance racing toward them. He tossed and turned in anguish, wondering if he would ever find relief from the pain that gripped his very soul.

When his wife got home and found him in such turmoil, it frightened her and she tried desperately to get him to tell her what was wrong. He alternated between uncontrollable sobs and a complete silence that suffocated his thinking. After a while he found himself sitting in his living room, staring and not saying a word.

But then, in the midst of his anguish, the phone rang. It was the parents of the girl he had run over. They had called to see if he was doing okay. Their toddler had died only hours before, yet they were concerned about how Amos was doing. He told them he was getting by, doing okay, but really he wasn't. He didn't know how he could work through the feelings of guilt that seemed to take his breath away. He couldn't imagine going back to work—who would know about the accident? Who didn't know?

What if someone didn't talk to him and he didn't know if they knew? He felt various stages of panic at just the thought of getting back into normal life.

"We'd like you to come to the funeral," the father told him over the phone, his voice trembling with emotion. "We don't hold you responsible in any way. It must have just been her time to go."

To Amos, the very thought of going to the little girl's funeral was preposterous. He could barely handle sitting in his own living room. There was no way he could deal with attending the funeral. "Let me think about it," he told the Amish man. "Just let me think about it."

After hanging up, Amos talked to his wife about what he had just heard on the phone.

"You know," she said, "you have to do what you know is best."

The more he thought about it, the less he felt like he could go. How could he see that little girl again, this time in her coffin? How could he look those parents in the eyes, knowing what he had taken from them?

Then came the day of the funeral. An old friend of Amos's stopped by the house to see how he was doing—he was an Amish pastor and had just come from the parents' house.

"Hi, Amos," he said. "Are you okay?"

Amos nodded, more of a shrug than anything else.

"I just came from their house—you know the funeral is today. They wanted me to let you know that they would really like for you to be there this afternoon, if you can make it."

This is an example of what I would describe as the ruthless

forgiveness of the Amish. They understand something about forgiveness—that the easiest way to forgive someone who has done something that hurt you is to get to know him, get close to him, because when you get to know someone, you can see how he is human and how badly he is hurting, too. Consider the alternative—isolating yourself from the person who hurt you, a separation that allows you to imagine he is some sort of monster or robot.

After the pastor left, his horse and buggy plodding its way down the drive, Amos's wife turned to him with sad eyes. She couldn't bear to see her husband in such pain.

"You know, I really think that might be a sign that we should go to the funeral today."

They talked about it some more and decided they would go. Amos's son also went along.

Before the accident, Amos had seen the grandparents of the girl more than the parents, and he knew the grandfather pretty well. Sometimes, when driving his truck, if Amos spotted the grandfather he would pull over and talk to him for a while. Due to his health, the grandfather was being cared for by friends of the family in Maryland when the accident took place and was unable to return for the funeral. At the little girl's viewing, the grandmother asked Amos if he would drive down to Maryland and talk to her husband—the grandfather knew about the accident, but no one had told him that Amos was the driver.

"I don't think I can tell him," Amos said.

The grandmother bowed her head. "But he doesn't know it's

you. We only told him about the accident—we didn't tell him that you were driving the truck."

"Well, I'm terribly sorry," Amos said, "but you have to tell him. I can't. I just can't."

A few weekends later, after the grandfather had been told that Amos was the one driving the truck, Amos drove down to Maryland to visit him. As much as he dreaded doing it, he knew it was the right thing to do, but as he got closer to the home where the grandfather was staying, he found himself more and more nervous. He wondered how *he* would feel toward a man, even a good friend, if that man had been responsible for the death of one of *his* grandchildren. Finally, he arrived at the home of the people who were taking care of the grandfather, knocked on the front door, and was escorted into a room where the older man was lying in bed.

"Well," the grandfather said slowly from his hospital bed, his long beard reaching down to his chest, "I'd much rather have it be you than a complete stranger."

It is almost as if the Amish revere the passing from this world to the next so much that they would prefer to have friends involved in the process. In this case the grandfather felt some sort of comfort that the momentous transition of his granddaughter from earth to heaven had been initiated by someone that they knew, and not some random stranger.

A few months after the accident, Amos still struggled with his part in the small Amish girl's passing. The days seemed to drag on and on, and the nights felt dark and heavy with grief. Then a package arrived. The first time Amos looked through it, he couldn't quite comprehend what it was: a book with page after page of letters, all addressed to him. Then he looked closer.

It was a scrapbook—a pink cloth album with green leaves, filled with letters written to him from every family in the church district the little girl's family belonged to. The book was eighty-five pages in length, nearly two inches thick. Every single family wrote a note to him full of encouragement and decorated the page with stickers and hand-drawn pictures. Some of the typed pages were held in the album with flower stickers. Some of the pages had short sayings of encouragement or poems.

The letters told him he was not a bad person. They told him the little girl was in heaven with Jesus—what better place could she be? They told him that it must have been her time to leave this earth. And, most of all, they encouraged him to persevere through his time of pain.

Amos's eyes filled with tears until he could barely read the letters. Nearly every page was signed "From Friends," and then the names of each individual in that particular family were listed. One of the poems written by a family went like this:

Our thoughts so often go your way
Since May 17th, that tragic day
When God saw fit for you to be there
As Ruthie left this earth for Heaven so fair.

We do not understand why God planned it this way
That you were the appointed one to drive in that day

Just as God was softly calling, "Ruthie come with me."
He let you focus elsewhere, that's why you didn't see.

She was such a precious Lil girl
Oh, much too special for this world
Her parting has caused a great deal of pain.
But her loved ones all know their loss is "Her Gain."

So now with God's help you will all try to move on
And leave this all with God, He will help you along
But in our weakness we sometimes forget to Trust.
And to stand strong in the Faith is also a must.

If we want to join Ruthie someday in Heaven above
Where all is Peace, Joy, Contentment and Love.
Imagine her Life as a precious angel now
Playing on the banks of Jordan smiling all the while.

Or singing there, now singing in the angel band
Her voice so sweetly ringing out o'er the Heavenly Land,
And running through the fields of flowers that cannot be compared
The beauty and the smell, oh so fragrant there.

I did not know what I could write to bring you peace of mind
Sleep wouldn't come for me tonight so I took this time
In quietness and in Prayer for you that all might turn out right
Just live your life for God and be a shining Light.

Till some day when we can leave this world behind
To walk hand-in-hand into that Home Sublime . . .

On reflection, Amos still finds the Amish commitment to forgiveness difficult to understand.

"I can't imagine how someone can get through something like I've been through if they're not able to talk to the victim's family, or if they are being prosecuted," Amos said. "Because, as difficult as it has been, it just made it easier, being able to talk to the family and knowing they didn't hate me.

"I come from an Amish background and I still cannot comprehend this forgiveness."

There was no court appearance or drawn-out legal battle. There was no questioning the competency or responsibility of the driver—was he looking where he was going? Did he take sufficient care when pulling into the driveway? The Amish recognize an accident when they see one and treat it as such. The parents still grieve the loss of their child. But they made a decision not to pursue some sort of legal justice or balance for their loss—what equitable balance could a parent possibly receive for losing a child?

Instead they chose to forgive. And for Amos it meant he could escape the prison of guilt and move on with his life.

Buggy funeral procession passing the home of the shooter

CHAPTER TEN

"Maybe I Should Forgive, Too"

I N ALL THE chaos of trying to get the girls into the helicopters and ambulances, no one back in Nickel Mines knew for sure where each girl had been taken. Even when descriptions of the girls started coming in from the various trauma centers there was still a lot of uncertainty. Soon, though, the parents began heading for the various hospitals where their girls were being treated.

The parents of Anna Mae Stoltzfus were taken by police cruiser to the Christiana Hospital in Delaware, where they expected to find their daughter being treated. But when they arrived and saw the girl, they knew immediately that it wasn't Anna Mae. Instead, they learned that Anna Mae had died at the school.

Just as the full weight of this realization began to sink in, the parents of Mary Liz and Lena Miller were escorted to that very same hospital. The girl that had at first been identified as Anna Mae in the hospital was in fact Mary Liz. The four parents wept together, caught up in a storm of emotions and grief. Mary Liz's parents, whose other daughter Lena was also in critical condition at another hospital, then rushed inside to see their daughter.

They walked quickly through the hospital's halls, passing room after room, perhaps still not quite believing that they would find their daughter there. Life-support machines beeped and hummed and set off occasional alarms. The seriousness that always abounds in such places weighed heavily on their shoulders.

As they approached the critical care unit, where they had learned Mary Liz was being treated, a doctor told them their daughter was on life support. The doctor told them that Mary Liz "was in grave condition and brain dead . . . and isn't going to get any better."

As they struggled with what to do, they received a call from the Hershey Medical Center, located about seventy-five miles away, regarding Lena—she too was on life support, with a prognosis similar to her sister's. It was now 10:00 p.m. The parents asked the doctors in Hershey to wait until they got there before doing anything.

They made their final decision regarding Mary Liz and sat by her bed until a little after midnight, when she was taken off life support. Her parents kissed her good-bye and told her that they were going to go to take her sister off life support so that "you can go ahead into heaven together."

I cannot imagine that seventy-five-mile trip from Newark, Delaware, to Hershey, Pennsylvania. Those parents had just said good-bye to one daughter and were on their way to another sad farewell. The car's wheels must have hummed incessantly in the silence created by their grief. They arrived in Hershey around 2:00 a.m. After they saw Lena one final time, she was soon disconnected from life support. She passed quickly as they held her.

Lena was the last of the five girls to go. The other five girls, in various conditions at hospitals throughout the area, would miraculously survive the close-range shooting.

Meanwhile, at home I slept a fitful sleep. Thoughts of Angie and Sonny plagued my mind, and I couldn't stop thinking about all of those Amish parents and the incredibly difficult path ahead of them. I also couldn't help being amazed at their strength and how their stories of forgiveness were already spreading.

MY WIFE and I drove through the autumn dusk to the Millers' house. It was only a few days after they lost Mary Liz and Lena. We knew the mother's brother—these were the only parents who had lost children to which we had a connection—and we wanted to offer our condolences, so we got in our car and headed to their farm in Georgetown for the viewing. Georgetown is just about a mile south of Nickel Mines, on Mine Road.

There were a number of cars there, which was slightly unusual, but there were also some plain vans, which usually indicates that some Amish had come from farther away—they hire drivers to take them from here to there if the distance is too far for their horse and buggies to travel. A lot of people made their way toward the house, and many were also mingling outside, talking to one another, coming and going.

We walked into the house, and I immediately felt the tradition and culture in the atmosphere. The proper thing to do when you arrive at a gathering like this is to walk around the circle of family, shaking everyone's hand and introducing yourself. Their interest always seems peaked when a non-Amish person arrives. Most of them knew who I was when I told them I was a Beiler and gave them my father's and grandfather's first names. They would nod and smile, immediately making the connection as to why we were there. This sense of community can be uncanny, the way they can keep track of generations in their head. It is an interconnectedness I have not encountered anywhere else in the world.

The women sat in a line on one side of the room, the men on the other, and where their lines met sat the mother and father. My wife and I spotted the mother immediately—she looked so sad, gaunt from lack of sleep and loss of appetite, and she was holding a younger child in her lap. The father sat beside her, looking very somber and worn. They would occasionally turn to the family members beside them and say a few words or would address those making their way through the line, but it was easy to see that grief had struck them to the core.

We shook everyone's hand, drawing closer to the parents through the crowd of sixty or seventy people present in the house.

The gas lanterns were lit, casting a subdued glow on the gathering and humming their usual smallest of sounds, like what you hear when you put your ear in a large seashell. As we came to the parents I felt a large lump in my throat. I remembered sitting in their spot, seeing new people come through the door, shaking their hands as they offered their condolences regarding Angie's passing. I remembered sometimes thinking that those people had no idea how I felt.

I reached down to shake their hands and nodded to them respectfully.

Anne spoke first.

"I'm Anne Beiler," she said quietly, speaking in Pennsylvania Dutch. "I know you don't know who I am, but we wanted to come because we lost a little girl many years ago. We understand how you feel. I didn't lose my little girl like you did, that part I don't understand, but I understand the loss that you are feeling right now."

We went around the other side of the half-circle shaking the men's hands. When we finished, Anne turned to the side and wept. It was too much for her, these memories of losing Angie and the sight of this poor mother in such pain, having lost two girls. I hugged her for a moment, and then we mingled with the crowd for a little while.

One of the family members we knew pulled us aside and asked if we would like to see the girls, so we followed him into a sort of receiving room, like a parlor. Normally you do not go in to view the body unless you are taken in by a relative. The room they were in would normally be the room the family used to entertain guests. But the space had been cleared for the funeral, and the only things left in the room were a very small side table holding a lamp, and the two coffins. There was no other furniture and no pictures on the walls.

One other Amish couple was in the room, and they stood silent beside us. The atmosphere felt overwhelmingly peaceful and quiet. You could just barely hear the hum of conversation through the doorway, but it seemed a million miles away. The comforting hum of the lantern was louder in this room, where no one was speaking.

The girls' coffins were arranged in a sort of narrow V, with their heads facing toward the windows and their feet toward the entrance we came through. The coffins were relatively simple wooden boxes. The girls' faces looked so young and peaceful. They wore white dresses made for them by family members. We stayed in the room for a few minutes, then left, taking our own memories with us.

We did not attend any of the girls' funerals. They are held very strictly by invitation only—and if you are invited you do not think about doing anything but attending. Since I have Amish family we have been to quite a few Amish funerals, and I am always amazed at how these services are designed to pass their culture on to future generations.

The first thing you would notice at an Amish funeral is how orderly everything proceeds, yet no one is giving orders or directing the service. There is no single master of ceremonies. Everything is done traditionally and peacefully. The entire service is conducted in German, not in their usual Pennsylvania-Dutch dialect, but if there are a number of "English" (non-Amish) in attendance the bishops will sometimes deliver part of the sermon in English.

The funerals are normally held in a barn, a garage, or a shed; wherever they can have the most people sit together. The benches are lined up in long rows so close together that when everyone is seated their knees will most likely be right up against the bench in front of them. The men all sit on one side and the women sit on the other. The body is in the coffin, placed between the men and women, in the center aisle and about one third of the way back from the front of the room. The young people always sit just behind the coffin so that they are the closest to it. The preachers and elders are seated first and up front, then the young people, and finally the younger married couples in the back.

Everything the Amish do, at funerals but also during any other cultural ceremony, is carried out in a way that shows the young people how it's done. Year after year after year, none of it changes: from how you sit to how you bring the body in to who sits where. The babies sit on their mothers' laps, and there isn't this rushing in and out with children that you sometimes get in our churches. Even the babies seem to understand that it is a time for quiet.

The funeral service lasts about two hours.

My sister-in-law, who also used to be Amish when she was a young girl, still remembers sitting on her father's lap during funeral services. Space was so tight that she and her father could barely move, but he secretly kept little pieces of candy in his shirt pockets for her, and he held her tight during those services. I am sure this is one of the reasons that Amish children are often so close to their parents, because of the repetitive physical closeness they experience during these rich ceremonies.

When I go to an Amish funeral, I still feel that it is such a part of who I am. It doesn't surprise me that so many of the young people choose to become Amish—only about 5 percent choose to leave. The traditions and structure provide a security and comfort that's almost irresistible.

When the service is over everyone files out of the building past the coffin, opened at the very end of the service for the final viewing. Interestingly enough, while the service is going on, the young men (who do not have to be told, but just know it is their job) number the buggies with chalk so that the family members can leave first. They take care of all the horses, unhitching them during the service, and somehow know which horse goes with which buggy goes with which family, hitching the horses back to the buggies after the service. Someone organizes that, but it doesn't seem to be talked about—it all goes like clockwork.

After the service there is a funeral procession, thirty or forty buggies somberly treading their way to the graveyard with a special carriage carrying the coffin. The graves are hand dug before the service. A normal grave that you or I might see in a non-Amish cemetery is dug with a backhoe, and the sides are covered with a drape so you don't see the rough edges. But when the Amish dig their graves they use a spade, and the sides are as flat as a board, with only the occasional crater from where a large rock may have been knocked loose. A wooden box goes down first as a liner, and then the wooden coffin fits inside that.

The coffin is lowered with straps by four people, two on each side. I remember at my mother's funeral how slowly her casket floated down into the ground. The grave is covered completely before you leave—for my mother's grave, my nieces and nephews were allowed to throw a few shovelfuls of dirt down. The remaining dirt is piled up in a perfect mound on top of the site. At the very end they put a stake at each end of the grave, and one of the stakes is marked with the date of birth and the date of death.

After the funeral, the crowd often will mingle around the graveyard, looking at other tombstones and remembering family members who had passed on before. Remembering is so important to the Amish. Sometimes they will visit these graves for quite a while, and there is a solemn air to the gathering as the living drift around those reminders of the dead. There is an immense peace in knowing they will someday be buried there with their families, but even more so in knowing they will join them in heaven. The Amish live very much in the present, working the land with their hands and enjoying good times with family and friends. But they seem to know more than most Christians that "this world is not my home."

Finally, after the service, everyone usually returns to the place of the funeral to share a meal. The day passes, and while the families grieve and miss their loved one, their family and community are there to support them, to remind them that the cycle of life will continue. This is the strength of the Amish community, this sense of support and closeness, and the firm belief that they will one day be reunited with their loved ones.

THE DAY of the girls' funerals came, and volunteer firefighter Rob Beiler found himself at Bart Fire Station once again. The men there were still reeling from what they had experienced. Most of them had not yet returned to work, so Rob and the Gap Fire Company had been handling calls in both areas while their friends from Bart recovered. Rob was the officer on the crew, and he had five men with him. Driving back over those roads, pulling into the station, and walking inside had transported Rob back to that tragic day once again. There was an eerie feel to the place and a sense of déjà vu. But he busied himself taking care of some odds and ends around the fire hall that the Bart firefighters hadn't had a chance to do.

For a while, Rob and his crew just sat in the hall, waiting for calls. These fire halls are so much more than emergency response buildings—they hold auctions, banquets, and community gatherings. The firemen have fund-raisers and serve meals in the fire truck bays. The fire halls are often close to one of the local churches and serve as central meeting places for many community events.

Some of the state troopers who had been at the schoolhouse the day of the shooting came back out to the Bart fire hall to honor the funeral processions that would soon pass by. They waited there, looking out of place without their uniforms. They looked like normal men, which in some ways they were, but there was also a quiet strength to them. Some of the troopers spoke to the firefighters about the event that brought them there, while others sat quietly, preferring not to talk about it.

A couple of troopers even had Amish children on their laps— they bounced the kids on their knees or gave them chewing gum. State police were talking with Amish women, something rarely seen, as usually the Amish men deal with any figures of authority. Rob shook his head in amazement. The tragedy seemed to be turning everything on its head, bringing everyone even closer together.

After Rob was there for a while he heard people gathering outside, so he went out front to see what was going on. It was a normal October day. The air was cool, and even in those few short days since the shooting, the trees had changed quite a bit, looking even more colorful. As he looked down the road he saw a sight that put a lump in his throat: a long line of Amish horse and buggies. The funeral processions had begun and would continue throughout the day. Thirty to forty buggies, sometimes stretching on around the corner, farther than he could see. The horses clip-clopped down the road at a slow, somber pace, and the Amish people inside, dressed in black, stared straight ahead. Sometimes an Amish man would look over at the fire hall and nod in recognition or tip his hat. The Amish had a great appreciation for what the emergency services had done on October 2. Each long line of buggies, led by mounted state troopers and a black funeral home vehicle, wound its way through the Nickel Mines countryside toward the Amish graveyard in Georgetown.

Each of the processions passed by the home of Charles Roberts.

The first funeral was for seven-year-old Naomi Rose Ebersole, the little girl who would sometimes cry before going to school. The second carried Marian Fisher, thirteen years old, the girl who had asked to be shot first. Finally, during the last funeral of that Thursday, Mary Liz and Lena Miller, the sisters whose viewing Anne and I had attended, were carried to their resting place. It was difficult for Rob to watch those solemn mourners pass by time and time again, undaunted in their determination to complete the ceremony honoring the girls' passage into heaven and into the presence of God.

As each of the processions made its way past the fire hall, people started coming out of their houses. Cars pulled over to the sides of the road as their drivers got out and stood there, respectfully waiting. All of the men lining the streets took their hats off. Rob felt himself getting more and more emotional as he thought of the five girls.

Members of a motorcycle gang came walking up the street in full biker gear, wearing leather chaps and black leather jackets, looking tough and very much out of place. But they stopped there beside the fire hall as the first procession passed, paying their respects. One of the guys came over and started talking to Rob. He had tattoos up and down his arms and looked as hard as a rock, impenetrable. He was the kind of guy you wouldn't want to mess with, or even make eye contact with. But Rob wasn't intimidated by tough exteriors.

"Where are you guys from?" Rob asked.

"We drove in from Carlisle this morning," he said quietly. Carlisle is a small town in central Pennsylvania, approximately an hour and a half drive from Nickel Mines. "We heard there might be some protestors here, so we wanted to show up and stand between them and the Amish."

Rob nodded his head in appreciation. He had heard about the possibility of protestors against the Amish lifestyle.

You can't judge people by the way they look, Rob thought to himself. This man had gathered together a group of his friends and traveled nearly one hundred miles round-trip to protect people he didn't even know. Their black Harley-Davidsons had rumbled across the state on a mission. The longer Rob talked to the biker, the more he was drawn into his story.

"This sure is something," the biker said to Rob as the processions continued going by.

Rob nodded his head.

"You know," the motorcyclist continued, "I had a son that was killed by a drunk driver seven years ago."

He paused, looked at the ground and shook his head. Rob could tell the hurt and pain lingered close to the surface. Something clicked inside Rob, a realization as to exactly why this man had come so far to mourn alongside the Amish. Common experience can often join people of extremely different backgrounds.

Then the biker looked Rob in the eyes.

"I have never forgiven the guy that killed my son," he said in a distant, solid voice that seemed to be softening. "Never forgiven him. You know what? Maybe I should. If these folks can forgive that man that shot their little girls, maybe I should forgive the guy that killed my son, too. Look at this," he said, gesturing with his tattoo-covered arms at the endless line of buggies rolling by. "Just look at them."

The two men stood there, somehow connected by the long procession. This type of connecting took place throughout the community that day, as nearly everyone stopped to reflect not only on the tragic death of five innocent Amish girls but also on the atmosphere of forgiveness that became more apparent with each passing hour, and on the Amish community's determination to remain resilient.

"Maybe I should forgive, too," the man said again.

Twelve-year-old Anna Mae would be buried on Friday, the last of the Amish funerals. She, too, would be carried in a procession of buggies from the funeral service attended by friends and family, down Mine Road, past the Roberts's home, past the Bart Fire Station, and would finally arrive at the Amish graveyard surrounded by a white fence.

The remaining five girls all survived, and after the shootings a local Amish woman would find small shoots of pure white lilac, a spring flower that had somehow pushed its way up through the fall fields and into the sunshine. Miracles?

Everyone looked for miracles in the days following the shootings, and the miracles themselves seemed eager to be found, waiting out in the open, causing even the most callous hearts to stop and reflect. As some of the visiting women had run from the schoolhouse just prior to the shooting, they glanced over their shoulders to see an angel resting above the school. The schoolteacher who survived the incident would have a dream that included a vision of her school filled with angels. And, for the skeptics, a more concrete miracle: one of the girls would survive a shot to the head, defying all the doctors' forecasts. Allowed by the doctors to "go home to die," she lived on.

Anna Mae's would not be the final funeral of the affair—on Saturday, October 7, nearly one week after the dominoes of that event were set in motion, Charles Carl Roberts IV was laid to rest. He was buried next to his daughter Elise's memorial in their family plot at Georgetown United Methodist Church. The sky was gray, and the seventy or so mourners gathered under a small green tent for the service. Charlie's wife and three small children, ages seven, five, and one, were there.

Approximately thirty of the mourners were Amish. They had decided that their presence alongside Charlie's wife was important. The men removed their hats while the prayers were said, then shook hands with everyone at the end of the service. Their outward expressions of forgiveness, at least pertaining to Charlie's death, were complete. But as one Amish man would say, they forgave, and when they woke up the next morning, they would forgive again.

According to a story in one of our local newspapers, one bystander—Bruce Porter, a fire department chaplain from Colorado who attended the service—was overwhelmed by the Amish support of the Roberts family.

"It's the love, the forgiveness, the heartfelt forgiveness they have toward the family. I broke down and cried seeing it displayed," Porter, who had come to Pennsylvania to offer what help he could, told the reporter.

He said Charles's wife was also touched. "She was absolutely deeply moved by just the love shown," Porter said.[1]

A photo accompanying that article underscored both the sadness surrounding the Roberts family and the empathy of the Amish. Far off in the background is a green hill covered in trees surrounding a bright white barn. A little closer are cornstalks the color of sand, standing thick and dry in the field, ready to be harvested. Then, in the foreground, there is a cemetery, and little Elise Victoria Roberts's heart-shaped, rose-colored tombstone with fresh flowers. Directly beside it, a fresh grave as of yet without any marking: Charles Roberts's final resting place.

Nickel Mines graveyard with satellite dishes

CHAPTER ELEVEN

Contend Valiantly

I F ANY RELIGIOUS group has a right to bitterness and retalia-
tion, it would have to be the Amish. Few people have endured as much injustice. A very brief glimpse into the
remarkable history of the Amish culture sheds great light upon
the forgiveness response of the Nickel Mines Amish community.

Their roots go back to Zurich in the 1500s, when a radical
group of Christians following Luther's teachings of salvation by
grace through faith became more and more disillusioned with the
Catholic church's teachings. One of their main doctrinal disagreements revolved around infant baptism. The Zurich group
didn't believe that infants should be baptized, as they were not
old enough to make informed decisions about following Christ.[1]

This was in direct conflict with the church's teachings and practices, and the group began to be viewed as subversive, one that could undermine the fabric of society. On January 21, 1525, the dissenters baptized one another in direct opposition to the state-run church. For all these believers, it was their second baptism, since they had all been baptized as children. For this reason the group was quickly labeled "Anabaptist," or literally, "second baptism." For at least the next century the group would be fined, imprisoned, and exiled if they refused to follow the state-run religious guidelines. Eventually they would be tortured, and even executed, for not turning away from their religious belief that baptism was a choice to be made by adults.[2]

Meanwhile, in 1536 a man named Menno Simons joined the Anabaptist movement, encouraging peaceful living, in contrast to one Anabaptist movement that tried to impose its new beliefs on others by force. Menno was so influential in the movement, and worked so hard at reconciliation, that by 1545 the Anabaptist movement as a whole was often being referred to as "the Mennonites." His peaceful approach to the doctrinal conflict with the state church influenced many toward nonresistance.[3]

In 1593, after numerous conventions and attempts at finding some common ground, a group of Anabaptists broke away from the main body over differences of opinion on how involved Anabaptists should be with the local, non-Anabaptist community, and how strictly the practice of shunning should be implemented. The main representative of this group was a man named Jakob Ammann. This group that joined him would eventually be referred to as "the Amish."

Throughout all of these divisions and disagreements, one thing became all too clear: the state church would do everything in its power to stamp out this growing group of radicals. Early on the Anabaptists decided that their response to this very real persecution would be nonviolent, even passive, favoring the rewards of eternity instead of the temporary, worldly ways of self-defense and vengeance. Their decision came with a high price.

Members of the Anabaptist groups were rooted out, tortured, and put on trial. Hundreds would be killed in all manner of cruelty: burned at the stake, pulled limb from limb, hanged, and beheaded. But through those early days they continued on in their beliefs, refusing to turn from their doctrine or their peaceful way of life.

Finally the Anabaptists discovered tolerance under the Dutch government. By the mid-1600s they even found themselves involved in mainstream culture again, something that worried one particular Mennonite minister, Thieleman Jansz van Braght. He feared that their new, comfortable life would lead them to forget biblical teachings on humility and simplicity, and the sufferings experienced by their forefathers barely two generations removed.

To preserve the Anabaptist culture of nonconformity, van Braght searched through court records and other documents for stories of Anabaptist martyrs and compiled them in a nearly 1,500-page book titled *Martyrs Mirror* (sometimes called *The Bloody Theater*). This book is still found in some Amish homes today, and among the Amish it is often referenced. The stories in its pages may have supported the Anabaptists in their commitment to nonresistance more than any other book apart from the Bible.[4]

By choosing a life of nonresistance, it logically followed that the Anabaptists would have to learn to forgive because nonresistors chose not to respond to slights or injuries or violence done against them. By passing down these martyrs' stories, they reminded each new generation that it is better to suffer and even die for the faith and to forgive their tormentors than to enter the cycle of violence that comes with trying to settle scores.

One of the most well-known stories from *Martyrs Mirror* is that of Dirk Willems. During the cold months of 1569, Willems, a "pious, faithful brother and follower of Jesus Christ," found himself being hunted down by the local authorities for being an Anabaptist. If they caught him, they would give him two choices: renounce his faith in the second baptism or be put to death.

They discovered his whereabouts and sent a "thief catcher" after him. Knowing what would happen if he was caught, Willems ran for his life, eventually crossing a frozen river. The ice was thin and creaked under his weight. Cracks spread from where his feet hit the cold surface, but he made it across the river. Looking back, he saw the thief catcher break through the ice and flounder in the frigid current.

Though his escape was now virtually guaranteed, Dirk couldn't let the man die. He ran back across the thin ice, stretched out toward the lunging arms of the thief catcher, and grabbed hold of his icy-cold hands. The two men struggled together against the river, the thief catcher desperate to be freed from the freezing water, Dirk pulling and hoping the ice would not break under him. Then they were both lying on the ice, their breath heaving, their bodies growing numb. But instead of rewarding his rescuer by letting him go, the thief catcher turned him into the authorities, who eventually tortured Willems and burned him at the stake.

Local court records corroborate the story:

> Whereas, Dirk Willems, born at Asperen, at present a prisoner, has, without torture and iron bonds (or otherwise) before the bailiff and us judges, confessed, that at the age of fifteen, eighteen or twenty years, he was rebaptized in the Rotterdam, at the house of one Pieter Willems, and that he, further, in Asperen, at his house, at divers hours, harbored and admitted secret conventicles and prohibited doctrines, and that he also has permitted several persons to be rebaptized in his aforesaid house; all of which is contrary to our holy Christian faith, and to the decrees of his royal majesty, and ought not to be tolerated, but severely punished, for an example to others; therefore, we . . . have condemned and do condemn by these presents in the name, and in the behalf, of his royal majesty, as Count of Holland, the aforesaid Dirk Willems, prisoner, persisting obstinately in his opinion, that he shall be executed with fire, until death ensues; and declare all his property confiscated, for the benefit of his royal majesty. So done this 16th of May, in presence of the judges . . . [5]

When an Amish father opens the pages of the *Martyrs Mirror* and reads aloud to his family about Dirk Willems, he is teaching them how to respond to those who treat them unfairly. And he is reminding them that even if a troubled man walks into a humble schoolhouse and kills one of his daughters, he can draw from the same rich reservoir of forgiveness that led Dirk Willems to show mercy to his own executioner.

During the same year that Dirk Willems was executed, a man named Willem Janss raced across the countryside toward Amsterdam. Only, in this case, no one was chasing him. Instead, Janss was hurrying so that he could attend the execution of a dear friend and perhaps strengthen him in his final hours.

But when Janss arrived at Amsterdam, the city gates were already barred due to the execution about to take place. Janss was distressed. His good friend, Pieter Pieters Beckjen, would soon be gone. Eventually he paid the gatekeepers a "certain sum of money" and made his way into the city.

Beckjen was brought out to face the crowd, his execution imminent. Janss scrambled for a better place to see his friend. He moved through the crowd, finally climbing the steps of a nearby building, and, as his friend was brought forward to die, he cried out with a loud voice: "Contend valiantly, dear brother!"

Janss was promptly arrested.

From there he did not have much of a chance. First he was imprisoned, then tortured twice, and finally, when he would not recant his beliefs, burned alive at the same spot where his friend had perished only two weeks earlier. The public record once again confirms the story, told from the government's perspective:

Whereas Willem Janss, from Waterland, residing at Doornickendam, present here as a prisoner, unmindful of his soul's salvation, and the obedience which he owed to our mother the holy church, and to His Royal Majesty, as his natural lord and prince despising the ordinances of the holy church, has never been to confession; and only once in his life, about eight years ago, to the holy, worthy sacrament; has further undertaken several times to go to the assembly of the reprobated and accursed sect of Mennonists or Anabaptists; also, about six or seven years ago, rejecting and renouncing the baptism received by him in his infancy of the holy church, been rebaptized, and afterwards received the breaking of bread three or four different times . . . and on the 26th of February ultimo, when one Pieter Pieterss Beckjen, bargeman, was to be executed in this city, on account of said sect, he, the prisoner, standing among the people, undertook yet to strengthen said Pieter Pieterss in his obstinacy, calling with a loud voice these or similar words: "Contend valiantly, dear brother."[6]

Contend valiantly. This is the heritage from which the Amish have built a legacy of peaceful living, nonviolence, and persistence in their faith. A heritage that would one day spare the life of a man in America named Cleo Eugene Peters.

On a summer night in Ohio in 1957, two men, both non-Amish, had recently been released from prison, and they decided to meet in Holmes County to rejoice in their freedom. As the evening wore on, something led them back to their old ways, and they randomly chose a home to break into and rob. It was the Mount Hope home of Paul M. and Dora J. Coblenz, an Amish couple, and, being Amish, they did not resist their intruders.

The men told Paul and Dora to get on the floor. Dora carried their nineteen-month-old baby, and the three lay there, hoping that somehow these men would simply take what they wanted and leave. But at one point, when the two ex-convicts were not looking, Paul made a dash for the door, hoping to make it to his father's house close by to call for help. One of the men, Cleo Peters, spotted Paul trying to escape. He raised the rifle he had with him, took careful aim, and shot, the bullet first going through the screen door and then into Paul's back. The two men then fled the scene, taking time only to pause over Paul's body and shoot him one more time, in the head.

They would eventually steal a car, drive off to Illinois, and shoot a sheriff's deputy before giving in to authorities. The Amish community was shocked and saddened. The story drew massive press attention as the world watched this normally insular community work through their grieving process.

Peters would be convicted and given the death sentence, a fact that left the Amish community feeling uncertain and troubled. For hundreds of years the Anabaptists had taken a stand against capital punishment, believing that, if given time, every human being may at some point reach a place of real repentance and turn to God. How would the Amish community treat Cleo Peters? Amish historian Steven M. Nolt recounts their response to this horrible tragedy:

God's forgiveness must be extended to all, they rea-
soned, and letters offering forgiveness and promising
prayer arrived at Peters' cell from settlements in many
states. Even the young widow, Dora, wrote to him.
Amish families invited Peters' parents into their homes
for meals, and church leaders visited him in prison. In
addition, the Amish called for a stay of execution.
Wrote one Ontario Amishman, "Will we as Amish be
left blameless in the matter if we do not present a written request to the authorities, asking that his life be
spared?" Individual letters and petitions arrived at the
office of Governor C. William O'Neill until the November 7, 1958, execution date. Seven hours before
the scheduled electrocution, the governor commuted
Peters' sentence.[7]

Then came a bright autumn day in 2006, the day when
Charles Roberts entered the Amish schoolhouse in Nickel Mines,
Pennsylvania, and shot ten girls. In the midst of this tragedy, even
the children instinctively lived out their Anabaptist heritage: the
boys, after their release, gathered behind the outhouses to pray;
the girls, bound and waiting at the front of the school, prayed
with one another; Marian said, "Shoot me first," and her sister
Barbie said, "Shoot me next." Years from now those phrases likely
will be passed along from family to family alongside the words of
another victim of injustice: "Contend valiantly, dear brother."

Two men visiting on the porch of the schoolhouse

CHAPTER TWELVE

From Forgiveness to Friendship

I MMEDIATELY FOLLOWING THE shooting, when Charles Roberts was identified as the gunman, a few of the Amish neighbors walked over to his house to meet with his wife and parents. Despite their shock and sadness over losing so many children, they were also concerned about Marie: Was she okay? How were the children holding up? Was there anything they could do to help?

It soon became apparent that Charlie's wife was also willing to do whatever she could to help the Amish families who were grieving. Both Marie's family and the families of the girls who were in the schoolhouse began to feel a need for a meeting. Such a meeting couldn't be arranged immediately—a few of the families were still spending quite a bit of time with their daughters recovering in the hospital, and the hospitals were spread out all over Pennsylvania.

Yet the feeling that a meeting would somehow patch this terrible rip in the fabric of their community persisted, and Brad Aldrich from our counseling center was asked to help facilitate the meeting. He spoke with a few of the Amish men whose daughters were involved, and they were eager for such a gathering to take place, but they didn't want it to happen unless all of the families could be there.

Two weeks later, in an event that went completely unpublicized, the Amish families impacted by the shooting met with the widow of the shooter. Marie and her parents, Charlie's parents, members from every Amish family impacted by the shooting, and a local pastor gathered together. In all, about one hundred people packed themselves into one of the Bart Fire Company's fire bays, where they normally park the fire engines. The group instinctively moved their seats into a large circle, with Charlie's wife and her parents clustered together on one side.

Prior to the meeting, Brad and his staff met to discuss their objectives. Obviously they hoped to see all the families experience healing and closure, but there wasn't a lot of professional literature that addressed circumstances such as these. There were plenty of models for the best way to go about doing forgiveness therapy, but most of them revolved around a prison environment where someone is going to meet with an inmate whom he wants to forgive.

We know as counselors that trying to guide people toward forgiveness can be extremely challenging and often takes a long time. The various models that have been developed by experienced and competent psychologists can be daunting. For example, one particular model, the Process Model of Forgiveness, developed at the University of Wisconsin by Dr. Robert Enright, has twenty processes divided into four phases. I am including only part of the description of this model so that you can see how complex and extensive forgiveness can sometimes be:

> The first phase of the process model is called the **Uncovering Phase** and includes processes that allow the individual to become aware of the anger and emotional pain that has resulted from the unjust injury. Consequences of the injury such as psychological defenses, shame, cognitive rehearsal, and energy depletion are explored. As the impact of the injury is revealed and validated, the choice of forgiveness can seem more possible.
>
> The second phase is called the **Decision Phase**, in which the participant can consider the possible continuing damage if he/she does not choose forgiveness and, by contrast, the possible positive outcomes of forgiving. This is a process where a person actively has a "change of heart" and chooses the virtue of forgiveness for moral growth as well as healing. The person also commits to the hard work of forgiveness over time.

The third phase of the forgiveness process is called the **Work Phase.** This phase includes grieving the pain of the unjust injury, reframing the wrongdoer, and deciding to offer goodwill to him/her . . .

The final phase is called the **Deepening or Outcome Phase**, during which the forgiving person begins to realize that he/she is gaining emotional relief from forgiving the offender. This is also a time when a foundational aspect of forgiveness is discovered: finding meaning in suffering. The person realizes that choosing the virtue of forgiveness as a response to the undeserved pain from the wrongdoing has indeed led to remarkable personal growth . . . [1]

Not exactly a simple process, yet Brad was about to meet with families whose lives had intersected through a senseless tragedy just two weeks earlier. What could he possibly expect to happen in just one meeting so soon after such trauma?

None of the victims or their families had undergone any formal forgiveness therapy. The environment of the upcoming meeting at the fire hall would not be controlled—Brad wondered if there was a possibility that one of the parents or grandparents would express any kind of anger or disappointment toward Charles's family that might be harmful. Whenever emotions like these are involved there really is no telling exactly how people will respond, or how complete their acceptance of the person involved in their pain will be.

Brad and his staff weren't exactly sure what they were getting themselves into, but both parties insisted it was time to meet. On the one hand, Brad knew he was in unfamiliar territory, and he felt somewhat unprepared for what might happen in the meeting. But he also realized this meeting was not his to control—God was orchestrating events. He headed off to the meeting fully trusting that God would bring healing to all the families as well as provide an opportunity to show the world how productive and healthy forgiveness can be.

Brad arrived at the Bart Fire Station, parked his car just outside, and walked through the cold autumn evening to the doors leading inside. The Amish were arriving, some in their horse and buggies, some walking. Harnesses clinked as the men tied their horses to the hitching posts, and the sounds of horses stomping and blowing steam through their noses filled the evening air outside the fire hall. The lights from the fire engine bays shone out onto the street and stretched into the darkness. The air smelled of burning leaves and other earthy, autumn scents.

The atmosphere inside the fire hall was subdued, but once everyone arrived there was a buzz in the air. Brad's staff began the meeting with a prayer, then opened it up for general discussion.

"This is your meeting," Brad told everyone in the circle of chairs. "We're not running the meeting. We're just here in case anyone needs us."

After some introductions, the family center's staff sat back and waited. For a moment, silence fell over the room, but not an uncomfortable quiet—it was almost as if, in that silence, the prayers of those present, as well as the prayers of folks around the world, settled into the room, bringing peace and comfort. After a few moments, someone cleared his throat, and everyone glanced toward a man sitting with Charlie's family, chair legs scraping as they turned to be able to hear better. Then complete silence again. Everyone waited with anticipation.

Charlie's father-in-law spoke first, followed by Charlie's father. Each spoke briefly with tears in his eyes and a catch in his voice. They wanted to convey both their regret that someone they loved had been responsible for the death of the girls, as well as their ongoing grief at having lost their own son. The air in the room was heavy, but not in a hostile way. It was more a time of grieving for all those involved, and the stillness in the room reflected everyone's heavy heart at what had happened.

Then the Amish spoke.

The first thing they wanted to know was how the Roberts family was doing. Brad was amazed at the depth and sincerity of their concern.

"How are your children?" they asked Charles's wife.

"How are you?" they asked her again.

And each of the families that spoke echoed the same sentiment time and time again:

"We don't hold you responsible in any way for what your husband did. We don't think your husband was a bad man—he was just confused and hurt and troubled."

One of the Amish men who had lost a daughter stood to speak. He cleared his throat and looked across the circle. Brad recalls that he was the first of the Amish parents who had lost a child to speak. If there were to be any tension, any discomfort at all, one would assume it would come from one of the parents of the children who had died. But as soon as he began to speak, any such concerns were immediately quelled.

"I knew who you were before," the Amish man said slowly, with tears in his eyes, "and I always recognized your husband. But I never really knew you or your family. I want to welcome you and your family to come to my home any time that you would like. I hope this will start a firm friendship between our families."

As his voice filled the room it became apparent that he was saying this to all of Charlie's family that were there, but Brad noticed a special connection between this particular father and Charlie's parents. After all, the Roberts family had just lost a son, and under such grave circumstances.

Both families knew what it was like to lose a child.

A chorus of softly spoken affirmation swept the room, as nearly all of the Amish present verbalized their agreement. They all nodded their heads in approval as a community, confirming what this Amish father had said and reiterating that what he had said went for all of them. There would be healing in the community, and their gathering together that evening confirmed that they were committed to becoming better people and better neighbors to one another in the future.

The meeting lasted an hour and a half. The sound of quiet crying could sometimes be heard. Tears ran down many cheeks in silent reflection. The men pulled handkerchiefs from their pockets time and again. But as the meeting went along, the initial uneasiness and sadness transformed into a communal type of mourning that felt supportive and unified.

After those who wanted to speak had a chance to share what was in their hearts, staff from the family center pulled out large tubs of mail that had been given to them by the small post office in Gap. The employees at the post office hadn't been able to process all of the mail pouring in for the Amish and Roberts families from all around the world, so on that night Brad and a few others helped distribute the letters and postcards and gifts that had been sent. Each family took two or three large bins of mail home with them, so great was the outpouring of sympathy from the watching world.

Several pieces of mail found their way to the school's teacher, Emma, from foreign countries. In order for those letters to have reached her they would have to have been hand sorted multiple times, due to the vague address scribbled on the front of the envelopes:

To the Amish Teacher
Pennsylvania, USA

Before they left, some of the Amish families gave gifts to Charlie's wife to take home to her children—toys and dolls and small crafts. Some of the very families who had lost children at the hands of Marie's husband wanted to give her a tangible sign of their friendship, wanted her children to have something that might ease the sorrow of losing their father. Empathy is the key to forgiveness.

Eventually everyone filed out and headed home. Brad got in his car, turned on the ignition, and drove those quiet back roads.

Some of those who lived close by walked along the dark streets. Others climbed into buggies and, with a quick "tch-tch" to the horses and a touch on the reins, were on their way home. The cold night pressed in around them all, but there was a feeling that lasted at least through the evening that, as a community united by forgiveness and compassion, they could get through this. They *would* get through this.

NO TRESPASSING *signs at the scene of the crime*

CHAPTER THIRTEEN

Why Forgive?

ALTHOUGH THE AMISH are often uncomfortable talking to the media, they understood why the press converged on their little corner of Lancaster County. From the beginning, they asked those of us who would speak for them to focus as much attention as possible on their belief in Christ. They saw this horrible tragedy as a way to bear witness to the world about the radical forgiveness they practice, which was learned from Jesus, who said of those who nailed him to a cross, "Father, forgive them for they know not what they do."

Thankfully, only a tiny minority of people will ever experience the kind of horror experienced by the Amish families of

Nickel Mines. But that doesn't mean that the rest of us will never face one of those instances where we have been so wronged that we don't think we can ever forgive who wronged us. In my counseling practice, when I have patients who struggle with feelings of guilt, condemnation, anger, or bitterness, I often discover that they have arranged their life experiences into grids of unforgiveness, and it is stealing their peace, literally draining the joy from their lives.

As I have observed the world's fascination with the forgiveness demonstrated by the Amish after the terrible tragedy that occurred in Nickel Mines, I believe I have grown in my own understanding of the immense appeal it holds. There is something about it that seems so right and so refreshing. On the one hand we are drawn to the outward peacefulness of the lives of the Amish, and the way that tranquility is reflected in their dealings, even with those who hurt them the most. But their story also catches our attention because each one of us holds too tightly to grudges or wrongs that have been done to us. When we see the way the Amish let go of wrongs done to them, we subconsciously think, "What if?" What if I could release some of my old burdens and pains? What if I could be free of this bitterness and anger that have had their claws stuck in me for years and years, until even the person who hurt me is dead or long gone?

Could I forgive the way those Amish people forgive?

The simple answer is yes. No matter what your circumstances, radical, complete forgiveness is possible. But it's not easy. The Amish have a five-hundred-year tradition of forgiveness, passed down and modeled from generation to generation, yet even for them it is a choice that they must sometimes repeat daily, such is its difficulty. The rest of us live in a world where popular culture glorifies "payback" and vengeful retribution. If I so much as stub my toe in your home, you better have a good lawyer—that's the message that tends to influence us more than the message of forgiveness that we have seen in this story.

Through the years, forgiveness has become one of the most misunderstood concepts of human interaction. Phrases like "forgive and forget" misrepresent the true meaning of, and work that goes into, forgiveness. It deludes people into thinking that forgiveness is supposed to be easy. Say the magic words and all the hurt goes away. You may be able to forget some small wrong against you, but most likely you will never forget life's deepest hurts, betrayals, or disappointments, even after you are able to forgive the person who caused them. The parents of those Amish girls will never be able to forget what happened.

Then there is the perception that forgiveness is only for the weak or the poor, those without the ability or resources or wherewithal to defend themselves. After all, "an eye for an eye" is the attitude constantly touted in our society as just and fair. If someone takes something from you, then you must take it back, whatever the cost. If someone wrongs you, then you should fight back. If someone fails to protect you or warn you or side with you, then he is liable. But forgiveness isn't just for the weak. In fact, I would argue it is only for the strong. True forgiveness is a courageous and unnatural act, while unforgiveness is an easy journey down the path of least resistance. It takes little strength to let grudges smolder; extinguishing them through forgiveness is a lot harder, yet so much more rewarding.

Yet these inaccuracies regarding forgiveness have persisted and have cost our culture and our hearts dearly. When counseling people who have been violated by others, I begin by giving them a more accurate view of what forgiveness really is:

- Forgiveness is a decision to release yourself from anger, resentment, hate, or the urge for revenge despite the injury you suffered
- Forgiveness is letting go of hope for a different past[1]

Think about the Nickel Mines school shooting in light of these two definitions. What could the Amish have done in response to the shooting that would have been a perfect example of living in unforgiveness? They could have allowed their anger or resentment for what had happened to separate them from Charles Roberts's family. They could have allowed hate to build up in them to the point where they would be consumed by bitterness and ill will toward Charles Roberts or God. In an extreme response, they could have allowed their desire for revenge to manifest itself in violence toward the Roberts family or other people outside the Amish community.

As someone who has lost a child, I find the second definition, letting go of hope for a different past, especially poignant. It would have been so easy, after losing Angie, for me to have become overwhelmed by the things I could have done differently, or that others could have done differently, which would have allowed us to avoid that heartbreaking loss. What if I had stayed home that morning? What if my wife hadn't let Angie go outside? What if my father-in-law could have gotten my sister-in-law's attention before she backed up the tractor?

By clinging to the idea that the past could have been different, I am suddenly dwelling on all of the people involved in Angie's accident and the small part they each played. This will always leave a crack in the door for unforgiveness to enter my heart. Until we let go of that hope of a different past, it will be difficult for us to move forward in forgiveness.

I've seen people spend a lot of time wishing things are not the way they are. This kind of activity is a waste of mental and emotional energy on something we can't change—mental and emotional energy that needs to be directed toward how God intended you to live today. If we let the energy we need today get used up dwelling on the past, we will eventually run out of steam. This is often why people, years after a tragedy or difficult experience, will suddenly suffer depression and other mental and emotional illnesses. How much mental and emotional anguish do we bring on ourselves by refusing to forgive, or being unable to know how to forgive?

As I have observed the Amish community, I have come to believe that, first and foremost, forgiveness is *self-care*. Although it's often thought of as something we do for the other person, it's actually for ourselves. True, when you forgive someone, you are generously offering that person an opportunity to be freed from his guilt. However, you really can't control how that other person receives your forgiveness. He might reject it, or it may take a while before he can accept it. But the second you forgive someone, you experience its benefits. You are relieved of the toxic burdens of anger, bitterness, resentment, and the like.

The Amish are so far ahead of the rest of us when it comes to this concept. They forgive because they believe God's way is the best way to live. They know that when God commands us to do something like forgive someone "seventy times seven," it is not a capricious rule for us to follow, but part of a properly ordered life that is intended for our good. They don't pass these lessons on to their children just for the sake of tradition, but because they want their children to be free of bitterness and anger, too. That's why it's woven deep into their culture. They model this forgiveness for their children, along with their entire belief system, by living it out, and they are able to do it so well that the next generation does not wonder how things like this should be handled.

When the families of those Amish schoolchildren chose to forgive Charles Roberts, it didn't help Charles. After all, he was dead. In fact, since he was absent from their midst, you might think there was no need to forgive him, but the Amish knew that by forgiving him they were actually freeing themselves from the hate, bitterness, and years of pain that would otherwise imprison them.

Make no mistake: if you have been wronged, thoughts of revenge and unforgiveness will want to come back from time to time, even many years later, depending on how deep the violation feels to you. Having the occasional thought of revenge after you have chosen to forgive is normal—after all, we are human, and sometimes we have feelings that we don't know what to do with or where to place. But it is important to understand that feelings are just that: feelings. They are not actions or choices. The best way to deal with those kinds of feelings is not to judge them. After all, people don't judge *you* by your thoughts, they judge you by the choices you make in life, the actions that you take.

We often judge ourselves by the thoughts that we have, and this causes a lot of unnecessary guilt and heaviness of spirit. What is most important are our actions, our choices. This is the part that I find the most unfair for the victim of a tremendous wrong— that person is the one with the long journey ahead. The person who wronged him is long gone and in some cases may not even think about what happened, while the victim is left holding a bag of hurt and difficult feelings that he doesn't know what to do with. The simple truth is that being victimized in such a way is unfair. It is terribly unfair that the victim is forced to decide how to respond to what happened. But life is not always fair, is it? And people are not always reasonable. In order to keep from getting deeper into bitterness and despair it becomes our responsibility to make good choices, no matter what has been thrust upon us.

In light of these facts, let's consider again these Amish families. When they found out that their daughters were shot, or killed, they may have felt as though they had lost nearly everything. Yet who was left with the difficult process of working through all of these painful feelings and emotions? The very people who were initially hurt, the Amish families. Not Charles Roberts. He was gone. But they understood that living a life of forgiveness is the only way to live, to truly live, and to choose otherwise would only hand them a life weighed down by despair and sadness.

IN ADDITION to the emotional and psychological benefits of forgiveness, people who forgive experience tremendous health benefits. Learning to forgive has been proven to

- lower your blood pressure
- improve immune system response
- reduce anxiety and depression
- improve your sleep
- improve self-esteem and sense of empowerment
- increase rewarding relationships, both professionally and personally
- reduce stress by releasing toxic emotions
- reduce dysfunctional patterns of behavior
- increase energy for living and healing
- improve relationships and social integration
- increase peace of mind
- aid peaceful death[2]

Maybe this is why the Amish are generally very healthy people. In a study done at the University of Tennessee by Dr. Kathleen Lawler, the physiological advantages of forgiveness became clear: after studying the affects of anger and hostility on the heart for more than twenty-five years, she started to wonder how people could avoid the side effects of unforgivingness. She began by measuring baseline statistics for adults, things like heart rate and blood pressure and forehead muscle tension (an indicator of stress). Then she asked them to retell their stories of being hurt or abused or mistreated. While everyone's heart rate, blood pressure, and muscle tension increased, the measurements for those who reported withholding forgiveness were 25 percent higher. Those who had forgiven reported fewer trips to the doctor for things like colds, headaches, and minor illnesses. Those who forgave were on 25 percent less medication. As more and more studies are done, it becomes increasingly evident that forgiveness is a key to long-term physical and mental health.[3]

The data keep coming in. And it all points to one conclusion: forgiveness is one of the most important things you can do for your long-term health and quality of life.

Forgiveness is good medicine, but it's not always easy to take.

Amish buggy continuing down the road

CHAPTER FOURTEEN

Edit Your History[1]

ANNE AND I were living in a Texas town where my family lived. It was during the winter of 1981. Over six years had passed since the death of our daughter, but the relationship between my wife and me had never been the same. A quietness had grown between us, and both of us seemed to mourn Angie's passing in our own individual ways. We didn't realize it at the time, but we had been isolating each other for all those years. I would later learn as a counselor that, often, the death of a child puts tremendous stress on a marriage.

On one particular day, Anne came out to the body shop where I worked.

"Jonas," she said, "I have something to tell you."

She looked gaunt with worry.

"You know the things being said about some of the women at our church?" she asked.

Recently there had been some disturbing rumors about the pastor and some of the ladies in the church, specifically that he had been having affairs with them. I wasn't sure who to believe. Or what to believe.

I nodded at Anne that yes, of course I had heard the rumors.

"I was one of those women," she said.

My insides dropped. The foundation of my life was cracked from top to bottom. I knew things had not been right between us since Angie had died, but I had never imagined the hurt that Anne had felt, or the places that despair had driven her to.

"I'm sorry, and I'm a sorry person," she blurted out, before running out, leaving me to process what I had just heard.

I stared at the wall after she left, trying to regain my composure. There were other coworkers in the shop, and I can only imagine what they thought was going on. First I was shaking and pacing back and forth, then I just sat and stared. After making several attempts to regain my composure, I informed one of my coworkers that I needed to leave and probably wouldn't be back until the next day.

I drove to our house, not knowing if Anne would be there or not, and I remember going inside, frantically walking back and forth in the hallway, thinking all kinds of irrational thoughts. She was not home. I became disoriented. I found my mind going into some dark places, thinking things like "I could burn the house down and burn with it, or maybe I should just get in my car and drive off." I didn't think I could bring myself to end my life, but I had never felt so desperate.

After a period of walking back and forth, back and forth, I collapsed beside the couch and screamed into a pillow at the top of my lungs. My voice echoed deep inside me. There was this immense emptiness in my soul. My ego felt crushed, my manhood seemingly stripped from me. My faith was challenged like never before.

My wife continues to say that the day our daughter was killed was the worst day of her life, but for me this was without a doubt the worst day. I thought I was losing my wife, my family, and everything else that I had worked so hard for.

I can't remember how much my wife and I talked that evening, but because of the pain I was feeling my bedtime prayer was, "Oh God, please don't let me see the dawning of another day." When I woke up early the next morning, I felt this intense anger at God for not answering my prayer, for forcing me to live another day with that pain. I didn't want to deal with it, I didn't ask for it, I didn't feel it was fair, and I just wanted it to go away.

What people do when they are discouraged is crucial. Deep hurts and discouragement can drive them to behavior they never imagined or even thought possible. When I reflect on how I felt that day, I can completely understand how a person like Charles Roberts can get to a place where his pain drove him to destruction. There were things I considered doing that day, and in the weeks and months that followed, that I still can hardly believe. In fact, I can't believe I didn't act on at least one of them.

I went to work the next day and shared with a few coworkers and my boss that I had experienced something that had shaken me to the core. I told them I might not be myself for several days. Little did I know how much I would change.

On October 2, the day of the shooting, these memories came flooding back along with the memories of losing Angie. Reflecting on these horrific pains in my own life is what drove me to tears that day on my way to the King farm, where the Amish were congregating. I knew the hard road those Amish families had ahead of them. Making sense out of things that cut so deeply is not something that happens quickly. I know of no shortcuts in the grief process. What I know now, after all these years, is that at a time like that, when pain seems overwhelming, you have two friends: God and time. If you can somehow keep from losing your will to live, you can get through horrendous experiences.

In those moments, so soon after a tragedy strikes, what people need most is a friend to stand beside them. This is one thing the Amish people do very well: in just a few hours, seventy-five to a hundred people formed a wall of friendship around the farm where all ten of the families had gathered. They brought coffee and refreshments, and stood in small groups, shaking their heads, wondering how something like this could happen, some talking and some silent. Sometimes the best support is silent support.

The day after Anne told me the shocking news, after I got off work, I decided to call a counselor. His name was Cuby Ward, and he had recently spent the weekend at our church doing a couples' retreat dealing with marriage and family issues. I called him and, in a shaky voice, explained the situation as best I could.

I remember how his quiet voice had an instant calming effect on me; how his gentle words put me at ease.

I asked him if I could ever feel close to my wife again. To be honest, I wasn't sure I could. How do you ever recover from something like that? I felt that what had happened was so unfair and honestly wondered if Anne and I could ever have the kind of loving, intimate relationship we once had. But I'll never forget what he said to me and the way it changed my whole outlook. Cuby is such a wise man, and he was very careful not to set me up for any false expectations. But what he told me changed my life forever:

"Jonas, the only chance you have of saving your marriage is if you will love your wife the way Christ loves you."

Those words stunned me. If he would have said that I needed to love my wife the way that Christ loved the church, I might not have paid much attention to his words. But because he connected it back to me, it had enormous impact. Somehow, because of my deep faith and the rich tradition of faith in which I was raised, I reached deeper into my soul than ever before and found God giving me the grace to do things I never thought possible. Cuby helped me manage my smashed masculinity and assured me that my physical relationship with my wife could be good again. Before our conversation ended, he agreed to meet with my wife and me, together, in just a few days' time.

As I pondered in the quiet of my soul what we had talked about, I became obsessed with knowing how Christ loved me. My search for an answer to this question of Christ's love became a passionate one, to the point where my life was driven by these thoughts. It was the only hope I had: discovering how Christ loved me so that I could love my wife that same way.

I remember making that decision—one of those decisions in life that is impossible to forget. I decided that, with the help of God, I would love my wife and my children the way that Christ loved me. Life was never the same again. I could not look at my wife or my children, or anybody else for that matter, without wondering how Christ loved them. It's hard to understand how bad things happen to good people, but I've often said to my wife that this is just earth, things are not perfect here, and I'm looking forward to better days in paradise.

What I did not understand at the time was that becoming obsessed with God's love for me, and becoming equally passionate about discovering how to pass that love on to others, had a deep impact on my soul.

My life had been torn down but during the rebuilding I became centered on two quests: discovering how it was that Christ loved me, and discovering how I could be a conduit to express that to others. This quickly took the focus away from those who had caused me pain. It's amazing to me how one day I was so mad at God that I didn't want to see the sun rise, and the next day I had this escalated curiosity about his love for me. I think that's an example of the wide range of emotions anybody can feel in the midst of a crisis. You just can't prepare for these times.

I often wonder why people can respond to similar tragedies so differently. I contribute my response to the culture I was raised in. My parents were old-order Amish and taught me many of the life skills and faith-based disciplines that came to my rescue during that time of deep need. In my counseling career I've noticed that people in crisis who have had little or no stability in how they were raised tend to wander and flounder much more than those who have some stability in their background. I thank God for my heritage and treasure it deeply. I know that the outside world wonders what the Amish lifestyle is all about. The Amish certainly admit that they don't do everything right. But there is so much about the way they do live life that I would not want to change.

In the days following the meeting Anne and I had with the counselor, I remember thinking, "Now I will do my best to express this kind of love to my wife, and maybe in a couple of months this marriage will be restored." Was I in for a surprise! My wife, mired in that relationship, had never had a chance to work through the heartache of losing Angie. She quickly became preoccupied with that long-ignored pain and where it took her. She found it impossible to respond to me physically. She couldn't even initiate something as small as holding hands.

At this point I began to understand, at least in part, what her struggles were about, and she agreed to go for marriage counseling with me to a counselor in our church, Wayne Welch. He was kind enough to make himself available to us. Not talking about our feelings was part of the culture that we were raised in, so after the shooting, when I heard that the Amish mothers supported one another by talking about what had happened and what they were experiencing, I was glad. I knew what that would do for them.

I continued my journey to restore the marriage. Several

months later I heard my wife say to her sister that she was not sure what was happening, but she found herself being attracted to my spirit. Little milestones like that gave me the courage to continue to do the right thing. Somewhere in all that pain, confusion, and discouragement I made a commitment to myself: no matter how I felt, I was going to do my best to continue to do the right thing.

Then, two and a half years later, the landmark experience occurred.

We were walking through a shopping mall with our children in Tyler, Texas, and I felt her slip her hand into mine.

It was two and a half years after deciding to love her the way Christ loved me. It was nearly ten years after Angie had died— nearly ten years since she had initiated any sort of physical intimacy with me. You might think this was a small act, but for me it was huge. For a split second I felt nine feet tall because what I had hoped would happen was finally happening. But the next second a wave of humility hit me and I felt two inches tall—I realized that what had just happened was not about me but about Christ's love working through both of us. Both of us. Not just me.

It sounds like a great story today because it has a happy ending. But I have to be honest, we still have our struggles. The arguments and misunderstandings and insecurities still crop up from time to time, no matter how far we have come. In other words, recovering from something like this doesn't mean you'll have a "pain-free" marriage. I'm not sure that's ever possible. But restoration is possible. Whenever I am given the chance to introduce my wife, I like to introduce her as my girlfriend, my best friend, my wife, the mother of all my children, the grandmother of all my grandchildren. It had always been my dream, when we were going through those dark times, that I would be able to say that.

My dream came true because of Christ's love.

I HAVE counseled many people in my life. Even after they know all the facts—who they need to forgive, what forgiveness is and what it is not, and why forgiveness is important—and decide they want to forgive, there is always one last question.

How?

How can I ever forgive my unfaithful spouse?

How can I ever forgive my betraying friend?

How can I ever forgive that violent stranger?

How can I ever forgive God for what happened to my child?

How can I ever forgive myself for that huge mistake?

These questions get to the heart of the matter, and there is one way of looking at forgiveness that has been extremely helpful to me. Richard called it "editing your history." Basically, that means that instead of dwelling on our feelings when bad things happen, we need to *reinterpret our painful experiences*.

Through counseling and good information I realized that my wife was the victim of "abuse of spiritual power," whereas originally I had looked at it as a coworker-to-coworker affair. The two are very different. Over time I began to feel better because I could reinterpret what happened into a less painful conclusion with new and better information. Something I always like to remember is that we don't live with the facts of our lives; we live with the conclusions that we make about the facts of our lives. It's important to make peace with our past because without doing so the past will hinder our joy for the present, and keep us from looking forward with any hopeful or joyful expectation of the future. My wife has also experienced a perfect example of this kind of reinterpretation. For years after our relationship was restored, she walked around with these feelings of guilt that she hadn't been a good mother to the girls during the difficult times we had following Angie's death. She simply could not forgive herself for what she saw as a period of mistreatment or neglect of our two daughters.

I would constantly tell her, "Honey, it wasn't that bad. I was there, too. You were a good mother to our girls. Your feelings of guilt and condemnation are not based on truth." Still, she couldn't discard them. She could not forgive herself.

After my mother passed away we were going through some of her things in my parents' house. We stumbled upon ten years' worth of letters from Anne to my mother. We didn't have enough money when we lived in Texas to be making long distance phone calls to Pennsylvania very often, which at the time were rather expensive. In addition, my parents did not have the convenience of a telephone in the house because they were old-order Amish. So Anne would send a letter to my mother just about every week detailing our daughters' lives. And there they were, all of these letters, all of those years.

I was sitting in a neighboring room as my wife read through these letters with one of our daughters. They would laugh when they read about something silly my daughter did when she was six, and they would cry as some of the old emotions came back.

"Today, LaVale dove off the high dive at the pool for the first time."

"Today the girls and I made cookies for the neighbors."

It was a beautiful moment. And in that moment, Anne realized she was not a terrible mother. In fact, she was a very good mother. This enabled her not only to see the truth regarding her mothering skills, but it also allowed her to continue the process of forgiving herself for the things she had done in the past.

This is what I mean when I say reinterpreting painful experiences or reinterpreting the past. The past doesn't change. Just the way we look at it. This had been a ten-year period during which Anne felt absolutely horrible about her mothering. Ten years about which she could only see the bad things because she was preoccupied with the struggles in her life. Reading through the letters she sent to my mother helped her understand that not everything in that ten-year time frame was as bad as she thought. Being able to see this period in a different light, through those letters, was key to her eventually forgiving herself.

Note that the history did not change, but her interpretation of it did. Everything has three ways in which it can be interpreted: the way I see it, the way you see it, and the way it really is. So it becomes necessary to come to a new understanding of what really took place. That often means getting new perspective on the events. One of the best ways to gather new perspective is to talk to family members, friends, counselors, or to God in prayer.

I also remember times when I felt like so much of life was wasted because I felt betrayed by people I trusted. I thought my pastor was my best friend, and I looked up to him and trusted him as my spiritual mentor. I knew our marriage wasn't perfect after Angie died but I still felt hopeful. Yet I later discovered that other people knew about the pastor's relationship with my wife before I did! I felt completely betrayed. But, through an effort to edit my history, I can walk back through those years I once felt were wasted and pick out a few flowers to enjoy.

Another example of this occurred when I was growing up. My family was not quick to hug one another or express love and affection. Somewhere in my early thirties I began to wonder why my dad never told me that he loved me. I just don't remember ever hearing that. I never doubted his love for me—that wasn't the issue. But I began to feel a little bit disappointed that he had never expressed it to me in words.

It is in these seemingly small thoughts or memories or emotions that unforgiveness can be quick to jump in. And this is where it can be very important to reinterpret these painful memories or experiences. I am not talking about lying to ourselves about what has happened, but about reinterpreting the facts.

One day I overheard my dad talking to someone. He said he couldn't understand how people used the word "love" so loosely. They love their house. They love ice cream.

"I might like those things, but I don't love them," I heard him say. "I reserve the word 'love' for God."

It suddenly dawned on me that my dad had such a high view of God, the word "love" couldn't be used for the things of this earth. I allowed this small piece of information to help me reinterpret my past. I realized that my dad just couldn't bring himself to love anyone but God, but that didn't mean he didn't care deeply for me. All kinds of healing took place inside me at that moment—the experience didn't change, but the way I looked at it did. If I were choosing to live a life of unforgiveness I could have easily shrugged off that information or thought to myself that it still didn't make up for a childhood of never hearing "I love you." But I didn't do that. I allowed that new understanding to change the way I looked at my father and my childhood. It was an extremely healthy moment for me.

The Amish are quick to edit their history. Only hours after Charles Roberts was identified as the shooter, I heard some Amish men saying things like, "He must have been very sick to have done something like this." They were not standing around basking in their anger or hate, saying things like, "If he was here right now I'd beat him to within an inch of his life." They weren't accusing Charles's family of somehow being responsible. They chose to interpret history in a way that allowed them to have sympathy for Charles and his family.

Forgiveness is a choice that the Amish people made, but I know by hearing from these families that dealing with the emotional aftermath of October 2 is a long process. Tragedy changes you. Things will never be the same. But I think the Amish people give us an example of a determined culture trying to make the most out of a horrible situation. And, believe me, that takes time.

These days our culture seems completely based around fast food and instant this and quick-fix that, and sometimes that interferes with the healing process. We think if one counseling session or a couple of quick prayers haven't changed our feelings for us then there must be something really wrong, something that cannot change. But there are no right or wrong feelings, there is no right or wrong way to feel when tragedies come our way. We feel what we feel because we are human beings.

Many people ask me, if they have truly forgiven, why can't they forget what happened? Why don't they feel any different than they did before? My sister-in-law, who was operating that tractor when our daughter was killed, offers a helpful alternative to the old Sunday-school adage "forgive and forget." "No," she says. "We forgive because we cannot forget."

We may wish these painful memories would go away, but the truth is that they won't. But when you can give horrible things that happen to you a less painful interpretation through a process of talking to your friends, prayer, and counseling, you can reinterpret your experiences to a less painful conclusion and begin to feel better over time.

Little girl exploring grass

⸺∽⠿∽⸺

CHAPTER FIFTEEN

Let the New Grass Grow

G ates *wide open.*

Let's think back to the scene my wife saw after driving those backcountry roads shortly after the shooting took place—back to that school gate, wide open and unlocked. Nothing could better symbolize the Amish community's forgiving response to the death of their daughters, or their determination not to let a tragedy isolate them from their neighbors.

But for anyone who still finds such forgiveness difficult to believe, or who still sees the Amish as unemotional stoics, there are also other images from those days. After all, the Amish are regular people, just like you and me. They still felt immense pain, in spite of their decision to forgive. Their children were still hurting from what they had experienced. And they all still had a difficult question to resolve: What should they do with the school?

Some wondered if having the children go back to the same school would help them in their emotional recovery; others felt the building represented too many painful memories, too many toxic images, and should be torn down. The parents of the school-children thought long and hard, and in the end decided a fresh start was what everyone needed.

Before the sun came up on Thursday, October 12—just ten days after the shootings—an outside demolition crew arrived. Under the menacing glare of two or three spotlights, the building was bulldozed, the concrete blocks and cement floor slabs broken up and carried away in dump trucks. In one photo that I saw, the claw of a large Caterpillar tractor reached inside the roof and peeled it back like the lid of a tin can, while a smaller bulldozer worked around the back, scooping up debris. In the background, only darkness. Soon the school was nothing more than a pile of rubble, with police tape and "No Trespassing" signs threading their way through the crushed cinder blocks.

The hole left by the removed foundation was leveled with the surrounding grass. The perimeter wood fence was disassembled. The next morning a lone Amish man raked the dirt flat, evening out the deep tracks left by the heavy machinery. His straw hat and black clothing blended in with the soil and the surrounding fields of short grass and corn stubble.

Only the trees remained, and the grass and weeds would

quickly grow over the rich, brown dirt. By the next spring no stranger would know a building had been there—the surrounding fields grew in and over what was once the school's property. Six months later, when passing through the area, even I, a local, had trouble figuring out where the school had been.

AT THE end of the school year, sometime in April 2007, on a clear spring day, the Amish invited Vietta and Samantha, along with some of the medevac helicopter crew members, to the school's year-end picnic. When Vietta drove up to the school, her breathing felt deliberate, her heart rate rising. By that spring she had already met all of the girls' parents, and she felt honored to have been invited to the picnic. Emotionally it was a confusing prospect—on the one hand, Vietta felt that a celebration was in order for the five girls who had survived; on the other hand, it was yet another reminder of the five girls who hadn't made it. She wondered how the day would go.

They were in their new school, with its paved drive, the building tucked away in the woods barely a mile from the old schoolhouse demolished months before. It was a more secluded spot, up a long drive and nestled on a hillside among some trees. The new school felt safe in its separation from the outside world.

All of the families were there, and Vietta even met the boys who had been in the school just before the shooting. She made the rounds, and all of the children were excited to meet her. She asked them questions about their new school and what they were going to do in the summer. The children seemed genuinely happy that Vietta and the rest of the emergency responders had come to their picnic.

All of the girls who survived the shooting were also back in school, save one, and even she had returned in her wheelchair for the spring celebration. Vietta found it hard to see her wheelchair bound, but also felt this incredible sense of the miraculous—this was the girl who had taken a shot directly in the head and, defying all of the doctors' predictions, had lived. Her release from the hospital had been widely reported as her being taken home to die, yet she lived on.

Vietta had spent much of her time the day of the shooting working on that particular girl, trying to save her, and here she was, still in a wheelchair. Vietta would steal glances at her and wonder if she could have done more. Or perhaps her work had kept the girl from passing. There were so many what-ifs.

The day continued and became one of serenity and peace and healing for Vietta and the others, talking and playing with the children, surrounded by the bright spring sunshine and the smell of freshly cut grass and growing things. Children's laughter danced around the school yard on butterfly wings, and it was genuine laughter, the kind that gave Vietta moments when she almost forgot exactly why she was there. Those moments didn't last long but were hopeful in themselves: perhaps someday Vietta and the children and even the parents who had lost children would live lives free of the intense pain that day had brought them.

Some of the pregnant mothers who had been in the schoolhouse on the day of the shooting had delivered their babies in time for that spring gathering, and they brought their own air of hope to the day. There is something about the tiny package of a baby, so innocent and dependent and new, that makes time pass slower and the world seem a much safer place. Vietta thought about Naomi Rose's namesake, now only a few months old. How would she find the world? How would her experiences in the Amish community, and its interaction with the outside world, shape her life?

There were eerie moments and difficult memories—some of the Amish girls recognized the first responders as the ones who had worked on them. The children would look up at them with a timid sort of questioning look, or a thankful smile. They remembered the first responders as if from a dream, or from a time so long ago it must have been before they were born. Emotions were close to the surface, and even the smallest of comments or questions could break through that thin layer of composure. When the tears occasionally came, they were brushed away quietly—they were not out of place, but it was not a day to let the overwhelming grief take precedence, even when some of those present still felt it.

Then the chopping sound of helicopter blades snapped the morning air. Parents cringed, children ducked their heads. The helicopters passed overhead once, then circled around and hovered above the school. The sound seemed so out of place in that new environment of safety and new beginnings. Even seasoned first responders could no longer hear the rhythmic sound of the blades without being transported back six months.

Get those helicopters on the ground!

We need stretchers!

Quick, these two girls first!

The helicopter landed close to the new Amish school, and as the blades slowed, and finally came to an easy stop, everyone found it easier to breathe. Smiles returned. Some of the children ran the short distance to the waiting helicopter. The crew who had flown the helicopter on the day of the shooting were off work and had been able to drive to the picnic—the crew that landed the helicopter could afford only a quick visit, but they allowed the Amish schoolchildren to climb inside, handle the controls, pretend to fly.

Six months before, some of those children had been loaded into the helicopters, strapped down to stiff orange boards, straining to stay alive. The crews had not brought them aboard with smiles and soft words, but deliberately and urgently, wanting nothing more than to save their lives. But this was a welcome change, the way the children could climb in on their own, the way their nervous looks turned to wide grins when they sat on the edge of the helicopter, wishing they could fly away in it.

Soon everyone gathered close to the school. The children lined up, some looking nervous, others swelling with confidence, and sang some songs for the responders that they had been practicing. Their voices were a reminder of all that had taken place, yet somehow they were also the promise of a hopeful future, a promise of good days that could not be stopped by anything. As Vietta stood there in the sunshine, she was once again taken aback at the resilience of the Amish community.

When the children ended their songs they served treats to

their guests: ice cream and other traditional Amish desserts like shoo-fly pie and whoopie pies. Everything tasted homemade and fresh: the ice cream on the verge of melting and the chocolate treats, rich and sticky. It was a tremendous celebration of life, of service, and of one particular community's determination to continue on in a spirit of hope and forgiveness.

I DECIDED to drive by the old school grounds recently. I'm not sure why. Something deep inside me must have wanted to revisit a place that had symbolized both the worst and the best of our lives. It's hard not to mentally picture the chaos of that fateful day, but at the same time I am reminded that this tragedy has been redeemed by the powerful stories that will inspire and encourage others for generations to come.

The small "No Trespassing" sign seemed unnecessary, out of place. It's just a field. Why would anyone care if you walked across it? But to our community it is so much more than just a field. It is the place on this earth from which five small girls and a hurting man departed. It is a place that held so much pain. Yet, in the midst of that suffering, the grass grows rich and green again. The cycle of life continues. And where hate could have grown and flourished, seeds of peace and compassion have sprouted.

All because of forgiveness.

I often think about my own life, and what it means to forgive. I wonder if sometimes, when someone wrongs me, I hold on to that pain, almost as a monument to remind me how much they hurt me. Do I sometimes secretly enjoy those reminders, allowing myself the freedom to look occasionally on them and remember how that person was so wrong to do me that harm? The Amish were wise enough to tear down a "monument" that would remind them, every time they passed it, of the pain dealt them by one man. Am I willing to dismantle those things that have caused me bitterness and pain?

What about you? Remember what the Amish said when they were asked how we should represent them to the press. All they wanted was to see this tragedy point people toward Christ. Have you let the hurts you have experienced at the hands of others keep you from enjoying the abundant life God intends for you?

I hope visiting Nickel Mines has shown you that you really do have a choice when it comes to forgiveness. You can wear your old hurts like a badge of honor, dragging yourself and others into the vortex of bitterness and anger. Or you can take the high road, the wise road, and, like the Amish, tear down those old strong-holds, rake the soil free of the debris that reminds you of your pain, and plant new seeds of friendship and grace. It won't be easy. And it will take time. But if you let the new grass grow in your life, who knows?

Maybe your children and your grandchildren and even *their* children will follow your example.

It has happened before.

ACKNOWLEDGMENTS

Growing up Amish, I acquired only an eighth-grade education and later discovered that I am severely dyslexic. To say that I never dreamed of writing a book is an understatement!

The subject of this book has shaped who I am today. Lessons in forgiveness have taught me who God is and who I am in God. So first I would like to thank God for His forgiveness and for blessing me with a desire to know Him more.

I would like to thank my parents for being true to the faith of their fathers and for giving me living examples of forgiveness in action. The positive life skills modeled in my childhood home have carried me through the darkest of days. And to my sisters, thank you for always standing by me! And to my brother Sonny, I have missed your presence since the day you left this life to continue in the next.

To my lovely wife, I want to say thank you for responding positively to my forgiveness. By accepting my forgiveness, you completed the cycle that has led to our complete reconciliation. Thank you for taking your place beside me as my wife. Through everything, my love for you has only grown stronger.

To my daughters, thank you for your constant support and for the four beautiful grandchildren who bring me indescribable joy. To my son-in-law Russ, you are truly a son to me. To Angie, I think of you every day and will never forget your place in our family. Your absence is matched only by your influence. See you in Heaven!

To Cuby Ward, the fruit of your challenge to me to love my wife as Christ loved me will be revealed only in eternity.

To Wayne Welch, the wise and loving counsel my wife and I received from you shaped my life calling to counsel others.

To Dr. Richard Dobbins, your counsel and teaching led me out of the darkest time in my marriage. Your counsel saved my wife from her own despair and, later, my daughter from hers. I am deeply grateful to you for the investment that you have made in my family. Your life and teachings inspire me to learn more and help others.

To Dr. and Mrs. Tom Wilson, allowing us the opportunity to minister to couples in your church added immeasurable benefit to our own healing process. Your friendship and love continue to bless me and my family.

To Dr. Diane Langberg, your graceful approach during times when "the counselor needed counseling" has deepened my understanding of God, myself, and others.

To Bill and Gloria Gaither, thank you for the beautiful music that you create, coordinate, and orchestrate that has impacted my life in such a positive way. Some things can be said only in a song and I thank you for your commitment to the ministry of music.

To friends and family not mentioned here, thank you for your support and encouragement over the years. All of you contribute so much to the fullness and rich blessings of my life!

NOTES

Chapter Two: Nickel Mines, Asleep

1. Bill Simpson. "History Lesson . . . Nickel Mines," Lancaster County, July 2007, 34–38.
2. Steven M. Nolt, *A History of the Amish: Revised and Updated* (Intercourse, Penn: Good Books, 2003), 74.
3. Our sources for chapters 3 and 4 include information from Amish and non-Amish interviews and news reports. One of the most thorough summaries of the shooting is "Lost Angels: The Untold Stories of the Amish School Shootings," from the *Lancaster New Era*, the details of which are listed below. This twenty-seven-page publication is available by e-mailing lostangels@LNPnews.com ($5 plus postage; all proceeds from the sale of this publication will benefit the victims of the West Nickel Mines School shooting).

Chapter Three: Converging on an Amish School

1. "Feel Like Traveling On," lyrics by William Hunter (Public Domain).

Chapter Four: Point of No Return

1. "Lost Angels," 11.
2. Stephen M. Silverman and Tim Nudd, "Amish Killer May Have Sought Revenge," *People*, October 3, 2006, http://www.people.com/people/article/0,1541823,00.html.

Chapter Five: "Shoot Me First"

1. "Lost Angels," 15.

Chapter Eight: Think No Evil

1. Dan Collins, "Amish Forgive, Pray and Mourn," CBS News, October 4, 2006, http://www.cbsnews.com/stories/2006/10/04/national/main2059 816.shtml.
2. "Amish Grandfather: 'We Must Not Think Evil of This Man,'" CNN, http://www.cnn.com/2006/US/10/04/amish.shooting/index.html.

Chapter Nine: Godly Examples

1. Encarta Dictionary http://encarta.msn.com/element/features/dictionary/dictionaryhome.aspx.

Chapter Ten: "Maybe I Should Forgive, Too"

1. Associated Press, "Amish Mourn Neighbor Who Killed 5 Girls," MSNBC, October 7, 2006, http://www.msnbc.msn.com/id/1517 4741/.

Chapter Eleven: Contend Valiantly

1. Steven M. Nolt, A History of the Amish (Intercourse, Penn.: Good Books, 1969), 10.
2. Ibid., 12.
3. Ibid., 17.
4. Ibid., 20–21.
5. Thieleman, J. van Braght, The Bloody Theater or Martyrs Mirror (Scottdale, Penn.: Herald Press, 2006), 741–42.
6. Ibid., 831–32.
7. Nolt, A History of the Amish, 297–98.

Chapter Twelve: From Forgiveness to Friendship

1. Robert Enright and Gayle Reed, "Process Model," http://www.forgiveness-institute.org/html/process_model.htm.

Chapter Thirteen: Why Forgive?

1. http://www.emotionalcompetency.com/forgiveness.htm.
2. http://www.forgivenessandhealth.com/html/benefits.html.
3. Ibid.

Chapter Fourteen: Edit Your History

1. I am indebted to Dr. Dobbins for the counseling and mentorship he has provided throughout the years. The concept of "Editing Your History" is found in his books *Feelings: Friend or Foe* and *Invisible Imprints*.